CW00348410

ROBIN COOK

PRINCIPLES AND POWER

ROBIN COOK
PRINCIPLES AND POWER

John Williams

Indie**Books**

Robin Cook: Principles and Power
John Williams

Published by IndieBooks
4 Staple Inn, London WC1V 7QH
www.indiebooks.co.uk

ISBN   978-1-908041241
eISBN 978-1-908041258

Set in Times 12/15pt

Printed by TJ International, Padstow

Contents

Preface

This is the story of Robin Cook as Foreign Secretary, from my perspective as his Press Secretary, focused on the period in which I worked for him. It draws on notes I made at the time: not a diary, but reflections and assessments and notes to myself. I have framed these in a narrative which tells the story as it was, in my recollection, trying to avoid hindsight.

Robin Cook was Foreign Secretary throughout Tony Blair's first term as Prime Minister, from 1997 until the post-election reshuffle in June 2001. I joined the team, as deputy head of the Foreign and Commonwealth Office's News Department, in May 1998, becoming Head of News in August 2000.

The main purpose of this book is to recall an outstanding individual who has now been dead for ten years. It is hard for me to judge how Robin is remembered, having been too close to him for an intense period of his career to be able to see objectively. To a generation which has come to politics in the last decade, does it make any sense in this age of anti-politics to talk about political principle at all? I hope this memoir shows that it does, not by portraying an unrealistic hero who never compromised, but by showing that it is possible for a serious person to hold a core of principle while making the compromises necessary in a parliamentary democracy.

Introduction

On the night Robin Cook left the Foreign Office, he asked what I thought his future might be. I said I could see him carrying on in Cabinet for a time, but a moment would come when he would have to resign on an issue of principle. This was not clairvoyance. It was a reflection on the three years in which I had worked closely with the Foreign Secretary. He had at times been so close to resignation that it seemed, as we sat alone together at his official residence after the television cameras had gone, that this must be how his government career would end.

Two years later Robin resigned as Leader of the Commons over Iraq. His posthumous reputation stands deservedly high, as the man who resigned over the most divisive issue in the recent history of British politics. He is rightly seen as a man of principle, one of the few ever to have left high office because he judged the government to be wrong. Robin Cook was not unique in having strong views about what he believed to be right and wrong. The political trade is wrongly disdained for lacking principle, in my view, though it has its share of unprincipled individuals. Having spent eight years working in government after 25 in journalism, I would go looking for principle in a minister's office more hopefully than in a newsroom. Perhaps I was lucky to work for two Foreign Secretaries – Robin Cook and Jack Straw – who were not only instinctively straight, but thought deeply about their responsibilities to parliament and public, and acted scrupulously on them. Ministers face penalties for misleading the public which journalists do not. They have to apologise to the House of Commons and sometimes resign. The possibility of humiliation imposes a certain discipline, though not all ministers meet the standard. And though it is an unfashionable view, my experience is that there are some people who go into politics to achieve things they believe in, though not all of them manage to maintain that standard either.

One theme of this book is the difficulty of reconciling beliefs – principles – with the necessary compromises of government and the daily pressures of life in power at the sharp end of the relationship between media and politics. Compromise is a democratic necessity: only dictators need not trouble with accommodating others' views and decisions. In some careers, the pressure to compromise squeezes everything worthwhile from a minister, especially one who faces a hostile media. But not all careers end in the abandonment of all principle. Looking back on my time working for Robin Cook, I see a struggle to retain principles while making the necessary compromises. There are serious questions to be asked about any democratic politician: do they have a core of beliefs motivating what they do and say, and if so, how do they balance those beliefs with the limited possibilities available in government? Some admirers became disappointed with the balance Robin Cook struck, but I feel that he achieved enough of what he believed in to emerge as a Foreign Secretary with substantial achievements: not all that he would have wanted, but more than enough to justify the necessary compromises. I am not objective about this.

His principles were as raw as bare nerve ends. Add to this rawness a temperament especially vulnerable to hurt, and a series of wounding events that tested him close to destruction, then you have a Foreign Secretary whose tenure was a case study in the difficulty of reconciling principles with power.

I started working for him when his statement that foreign policy must have an ethical dimension had become so ridiculed that he asked: 'Am I finished? And no bullshit.'

I said no, he was not finished. I won't pretend I completely believed it; but I wanted to make it so. Our democracy would have lost something valuable had Robin Cook's government career been swept away before he had barely begun.

One

Life in the Shadows

Robin Cook was of a Labour generation in danger of never serving in government. He was past 50 before he opened a red box, though he had arrived in the House of Commons not yet 30. He was born in Bellshill in the Lanarkshire coalfield on February 28, 1946, the only son of Peter and Christina Cook, grandson of a miner of General Strike vintage. Robin made his first known speech in a school debate aged 11. His father was a teacher, who became head of science at Edinburgh Royal High when Robin was 14. There was an obligation to meet high standards for his father, but Robin needed no incentive. He thrived in a studious culture where brains and effort were prized, and became president of debates in 1963. He was already Labour and a member of the Campaign for Nuclear Disarmament.

At Edinburgh University, he took English literature, became chairman of the Labour club, arts editor of the students' magazine, and grew a beard. He was a member of the debates committee, where he met a medical student, Margaret Whitmore, within a fortnight asking her to marry him. He won the class prize but just missed a first. He became a teacher, but his ambition was in politics. Robin Cook first stood for Parliament in 1970, polling respectably in a Conservative seat. He joined the Workers' Educational Association – like Neil Kinnock – in 1971 and became an Edinburgh councillor, soon heading the housing committee, and impressing with a programme of providing thousands of indoor bathrooms. The slum poverty close by Edinburgh's elegant prosperity was to be a Cook theme when he arrived in Parliament. Robin won the nomination for Edinburgh Central as the left-wing candidate, and was elected MP with a majority of 961 on his 28th birthday. Among the activists campaigning for him was a brilliant young man five years his junior, Gordon Brown. Robin Cook increased his majority to 3,953 in the second 1974 election, calling for a No vote in the referendum on Europe which took place the following year.

Harold Wilson's second government led a precarious existence, in a minority from February and with a majority of three from October 1974. Jim Callaghan, who took over on Wilson's retirement in 1976, faced a sterling crisis, deep spending cuts and the humiliation of seeking a loan from the International Monetary Fund. Robin Cook joined the Tribune Group, then the home of the parliamentary left, and rebelled on economic policy, an independent-minded backbencher rather than a potential minister in a government struggling to retain credibility in the party and the country.

After Labour lost the 1979 General Election, Robin Cook was on Michael Foot's campaign team for the leadership against Denis Healey, the combative steward of the Callaghan government's economic policies. This was much the same trajectory as Neil Kinnock, who had entered parliament four years earlier than Robin. Both refused to support Tony Benn for the deputy leadership against Denis Healey in the 1981 contest which was the wedge that divided the Labour left. This was the period when Labour moored itself a long way from the mainstream in which Margaret Thatcher was given the freedom to win two more elections, while the Labour Party lost talents as big as Roy Jenkins, Shirley Williams and David Owen to a new centrist party, the SDP. After Foot lost badly to Thatcher in 1983, Robin Cook headed Neil Kinnock's campaign team for the Labour leadership.

Robin's reward was to run Labour's campaign for the 1984 European elections – a success from a low base – in which the party began its pirouette away from a policy of withdrawal. 'Reflation in one country is no longer a viable strategy in the modern world,' said Robin Cook, quoted in a 1998 biography by John Kampfner. At that time, with unemployment having quickly more than doubled to three million under Margaret Thatcher, 'reflation' was the word for the alternative, which the Prime Minister famously disdained. Her slogan TINA (There Is No Alternative) was surely one of the least democratic ever minted. The point of democracy is that there is an alternative which others are entitled to think is wrong. The only places without alternatives are not democracies. Labour was still not an alternative compelling enough for people to elect, and Neil Kinnock carried on after 1987 moving Labour away from its moorings towards the mainstream. The most painful loosening of political ties was to unilateral nuclear disarmament: difficult for Robin Cook too.

The Soft Left was mis-named, given its hard focus on what was essential to end the apparently endless Thatcher years. Some would quarrel with linking the word principle with left-wingers like Robin Cook and his leader, Neil Kinnock, who took this direction after the defeat of Michael Foot. But as John Maynard Keynes said, when the facts change, I change my mind – what do you do? (Often quoted by another Tribunite of the period, the future Foreign Secretary Jack Straw). The Cold War was ending, with Presidents Reagan and Gorbachev swapping hitherto unthinkable ideas for nuclear arms reductions. On Europe, Britain had too long been a member for withdrawal to be anything now but a 'last resort,' as Kinnock's leadership manifesto put it, dancing away from old certainties. John Kampfner describes it well, that Robin Cook would 'in later years focus with almost missionary zeal on hopes that the centre left parties [of Europe] would work together in common cause.' In France, President Mitterand had discovered that his mandate for left of centre economics counted for nothing without the rest of the Europe going the same way.

Robin Cook was – at a level below the highly exposed Neil Kinnock – convinced that Labour had to change and make itself electable. As Jack Straw liked to say, 'compromise with the electorate' was for some on the left a betrayal of principle. But principles are easy to have if they are never likely to be acted on. The test of serious politics is bringing principles to bear in government, not passing resolutions about them in Opposition. This is not the place for detailed assessment of Labour's internal agonies in the Thatcher years. But since principle is a theme, it is the place to challenge the easy sneer that politicians will do anything to gain power. If they were not prepared to do something to gain power, how would democracy work? Democracy imposes a duty on those who would govern to re-consider in the light of defeat, while retaining faith in beliefs that have not been decisively rejected by the voters or confounded by events.

Robin Cook was given a job that symbolised continuing belief in something principled, the National Health Service. As Shadow Health Secretary from 1987, his main opponent was John Moore, a name barely recalled now, but who might have been remembered as Margaret Thatcher's successor. When he was promoted to Health Secretary in 1988, Moore was widely regarded as a potential Prime Minister. Robin Cook's parliamentary performances stripped the Thatcher government's health policies so bare that Moore, unable to cope with his shadow's withering critique in the Commons, never recovered politically. This was the founding of Robin Cook's lasting reputation as the outstanding parliamentary performer of his time. As a long-serving member of the press gallery and a chairman of the political correspondents (the lobby), I have never seen any parliamentary bloodsport to match Robin Cook coolly hounding a minister. It is rare for a shadow to destroy a Secretary of State, who has all the advantages of being able to do things – make decisions – which the shadow lacks. The Secretary has the machinery of government to propel him into the Commons. The shadow has a cubicle office and a researcher. I remember going to see Robin when I was political correspondent for the London Evening Standard at this time. His tiny room stacked with papers was a small base from which to bring down the Health Secretary. He did it with facts as well as rhetoric, gathering evidence of shortages and closures which gave the Evening Standard correspondent a supply of page leads that discomfited the government.

Labour had become expert in this sort of precise opposition, hacking away at government credibility. Gordon Brown, by then deputy to Shadow Chancellor John Smith, was very good at it, as was the Shadow Employment Secretary Tony Blair, though I recall him being not quite so ruthless. Some mistook him for a lightweight, including some rivals.

Being a superb Opposition did not win Labour the 1992 election. John Major brought the Conservatives back from a huge deficit in the opinion polls to win narrowly. John Smith became Labour leader, appointing Robin shadow Trade and Industry Secretary. Gordon Brown took the chief economic job, Shadow Chancellor, having made his Commons reputation by taking on brilliantly one of the biggest figures of the time, Nigel Lawson.

Nobody realised that Shadow Home Secretary would be the making of Tony Blair. He turned fear of crime from being a Conservative strength to an issue on which people felt increasingly comfortable about Labour. He talked in a sensible, low-key way that showed understanding of people's anxieties, setting a refreshingly straightforward tone that became Labour's. The party seemed to be talking about things that mattered to most people instead of its own preoccupations, a change that was arguably as important as neutralising fears about Labour as the party of tax, or moving away from electoral liabilities like unilateralism. John Smith's air of massively reassuring competence contrasted with an increasingly disorderly performance from the Conservative Party, over the economy and over Europe. Smith died of a heart attack on 12 May, 1994, his legacy a long poll lead and a strong sense that Labour was to be trusted.

Robin Cook very much wanted to stand for the leadership, though as a racing tipster (for a Scottish newspaper) he understood the odds with painful clarity. A younger man who seemed to have slipped nonchalantly into high politics was the strong favourite, as if effortlessly. I was political editor of the *Daily Mirror* then, and close to the leading Labour figures as their main daily contact with the only newspaper that unfashionably supported them. Robin was frank in private that he couldn't beat Blair. He found this difficult. He knew that the way he looked was one reason for his acknowledged brilliance not reaping greater reward.

Gordon Brown found it difficult too. He had his spokesman, Charlie Whelan, insist that it was 'early doors yet', while anyone who knew the Labour Party at all understood that Blair was going to win, provided he ran. Blair was sensibly silent in public before John Smith's funeral. But when I asked him privately 'you will run, won't you?' he said 'of course'. After the funeral, Gordon Brown withdrew with great reluctance. Blair said to me: 'The Labour government will be a Blair-Brown government.'

Robin was reshuffled from Shadow Trade and Industry to Shadow Foreign Secretary, a fine move except that it was suspected Gordon Brown wanted him kept out of economic policy. There was throughout the New Labour years a mystery about why Gordon Brown and Robin Cook detested one another. I never found out a specific reason, a single incident or argument or insult that caused it. My theory is that there wasn't one, though I was not close enough in the formative years to know, and when the bitterness was causing problems in government, I was more interested in drawing the poison than inquiring after the origin. It is usually best in life to look for the obvious. Both were outstanding talents who knew how gifted they were. There can be only one number one. Robin Cook was not prepared to cede to a man five years younger and Gordon Brown was prepared to cede to no-one (even to Blair as Prime Minister). Robin saw economic policy – how you run your society – as fundamental to his politics and so did not take lightly being eased out of it.

So there were serious as well as personal differences, especially on how far to move in the direction of free markets as the key to economic success. Steve Richards of *The Independent* says acutely in his Brown biography that Robin was "...an unapologetic advocate of Keynesian economics when it was unfashionable to be so, seeing through some of the market orthodoxies willingly accepted by Blair and pragmatically celebrated by Brown. Cook could have claimed further vindication if he had lived, when it became the new fashion to challenge market orthodoxy.'

And then there was the Gordon style, which was ruthless, as I found when Brown was Chancellor and Cook the Foreign Secretary. Robin wasn't ruthless. And he did cede to Blair, with a realistic sense of himself as outstanding, but not destined to be leader.

As Shadow Foreign Secretary, Robin Cook applied himself diligently to learning his new trade. There is a nice story in John Kampfner's biography – relevant to what follows in office – of a visit Robin made to the US when Sir John Kerr, then ambassador to Washington, was 'astonished, not just by Cook's grasp of detail and thirst for information, but that two months later he phoned him to go over some of the minutiae'.

Robin's flair for grasping detail was the key to his finest moment in Opposition, his now legendary performance on the day the Conservative government published a report on arms sales to Iraq, in which Sir Richard Scott detailed over 2,000 pages how the rules had been serially broken. Though complicated, this episode was high political drama. It was necessary to queue from an early hour to get in to see Margaret Thatcher face Scott's forensic questioning. I was in the queue with Robin that day. He knew the scandal intimately. The government allowed him only three hours to look at the report's five volumes before going into the Commons, where he lacerated the Trade Secretary Ian Lang's defence (the job title at the time was President of the Board of Trade). Robin Cook, having used his three hours to mine the report for detail, highlighted critical passages that the President of the Board of Trade had not mentioned in his Commons statement:

'I did not recognise the report that I read from the statement that the House has just heard. The right honourable gentleman tells us that the Government accept many of the report's recommendations…. will he also accept Sir Richard's conclusion that that failure was, in his words, deliberate and the result of three Ministers agreeing to give that no publicity? [Hon. Members: "Oh."] It is in the report. Will he also accept the conclusion that the reason that they gave it no publicity was that they did not want the public outrage that would greet it?….

'Does the President accept – he did not mention it in his statement – that Sir Richard's conclusion is that Government statements on defence exports to Iraq, in his words, "consistently failed" to comply with "Questions of Procedure for Ministers" and thereby failed to discharge the principle of ministerial accountability?' ….

'Is the President really going to ask the House to accept a report which, over five volumes, demonstrates how this Government misjudged Saddam Hussein, misled Members of Parliament and misdirected the prosecution, then tell us that no one in the Government will accept responsibility for getting it wrong?'

It was the outstanding parliamentary performance of my time and I would bet that most political journalists of my vintage would say the same, not least because we were all incapable of digesting the Scott report at minimum notice, despite long experience of gutting official documents at speed. We knew from our own grappling with its dense text how intensely difficult Robin's speed-reading had been. In the *Mirror* office we used our Scott as a sturdy doorstop thereafter.

Tony Blair won the 1997 election by an even greater Commons majority than Margaret Thatcher had at her peak. Like her, he did it well short of 50% of the vote, but with a commonly accepted sense that he – like Thatcher – had caught the changing mood of the times. Blair was personally modest but politically aware that this was his moment, that he knew how to do politics in a new way – 'new' was the word. Blair was an electoral genius, burying the consistently formidable Conservative machine and transforming Labour's. His government might have done whatever it wanted, but he was oddly cautious for someone so sweepingly in command of the terrain for several years. It was as if Blair could not quite believe the scale of his victory nor trust his luck to last.

He appointed Robin Cook his Foreign Secretary and told his spokesman, Alastair Campbell, that they must 'keep a wary eye on him'.

Two
Before the Fall

The Foreign Secretary has a grand job but relatively little power to do things. The nature of foreign policy is that other countries' agreement is usually needed if actions are to be taken. This takes time and can be frustrating, the results a compromise or common denominator, or no result at all. And the job is less about taking the initiative than about reacting to what is happening in the world.

In May 1997, the new Foreign Secretary was able on his first weekend to signal a change in approach, which he did with flair in an interview saying 'goodbye to xenophobia' in *The Observer*. He made much of a routine meeting of European foreign ministers on the first Monday as a show of Britain's positive new approach. At their first EU summit representing Britain, Tony Blair and Robin Cook looked and sounded more at ease with Europe than their predecessors. These were changes of tone rather than by actions: a photocall with a young Prime Minister cheerfully riding a bike didn't amount to a strategic shift. But tone matters in foreign policy. Often it is the only instrument a Foreign Secretary has: the tone he takes, the words he uses, the sharpness or the blandness with which he takes a position, whether he rushes in or hangs back with a condemnation, challenges boldly or merely hints at disquiet, welcomes a development effusively or conspicuously says nothing. So issuing a 'mission statement' was more than publishing a glossy pamphlet issued with fanfare, it was an act of foreign policy. And it was different from making pronouncements in Opposition. It committed Britain to take a certain approach, with a certain tone, and bound the Foreign Secretary to live up to it. Had it been issued as a written answer in the House of Commons, the traditional way of making significant but low-key announcements, the words themselves would probably have had little consequence. They are – read now, in lifeless print – pretty humdrum: 'The mission of the Foreign and Commonwealth Office is to promote the national interest of the United Kingdom and to contribute to a strong world community.' The four 'benefits' to be secured were security, prosperity, quality of life and mutual respect. There is nothing wrong with government stating the obvious; better than over-stating itself, or than novelty for its own sake. But by laying on the sort of show the Foreign Office had never seen, Robin Cook was declaring boldly that things were going to be dramatically different and that he wanted to be judged by how different.

He was judged highly in the first flush of Labour newness in the summer of 1997. Hugo Young, veteran columnist of *The Guardian*, came in to see the Foreign Secretary for an off the record conversation on 29 July, and reached this verdict in his private notes (now published posthumously as *The Hugo Young Papers*):

> '*Cook was immensely relaxed, wholly on top of the job. Obviously rejoiced in by officials – as he is by Albright [US Secretary of State] and Blair. Still the same man – umpompous, witty, serious – swift. I have seldom seen a politician so obviously relishing what he had been waiting to do.*'

But Robin Cook's reputation was soon in decline. 'The apparent fall from grace was astounding,' wrote John Kampfner. For *The Observer* columnist Andrew Rawnsley, writing in his book about Blair's government, *Servants of the People,* Robin Cook became 'the Cabinet's figure of folly'. Hugo Young, back to see the Foreign Secretary on 6 May 1998, now noted: 'He no longer bestrides as he used to. This of course is in part due to his domestic chaos. But it is also because, as leader of the left, he has had every tooth drawn by the Blair triumph.'

Over this period, Robin Cook made a series of mistakes and/or was struck by one piece of bad luck after another, and compounded his difficulties with poor responses. It is hard to credit that a career which had for years gone from success to success could have hit such a run of catastrophes. It must partly have been because Robin Cook had had so long a run of successes that he was badly ill-equipped to cope with setbacks. Another *Guardian* writer, Martin Kettle, had described him as 'probably the most generally admired politician in Britain today' [Kampfner p115] just before the election. Such praise is poor preparation for handling the fall-out from mistakes.

There was another obvious reason for Robin's drastic loss of touch: the 'domestic chaos' to which Hugo Young referred. The Foreign Secretary's marriage broke up on Friday 1st August 1997 when he received a phone call from Alastair Campbell, the Prime Minister's spokesman and the whole government's handler of media troubles. The Campbell diary is painfully vivid. Robin and his wife were in a car at Heathrow, about to board a plane for their holiday in the United States.

'I asked if he was alone. He said no, I'm with Margaret and David Mathieson [special advisor]. I said, given what I am about to say, you might want to go to a private phone and call me back....I could now hear Margaret chatting away happily in the background. I said are you sure you don't want to find a private phone. He said no, you speak and I will listen. I suspected he knew what was coming. I said it's you and Gaynor [Robin's secretary in Opposition]. A freelance has seen you coming from her flat, having staked it out through the night, and they have pictures....I was, I must say, quite impressed at how cool he was.'

Tony Blair gave his Foreign Secretary strong support, Alastair Campbell worked to limit the media damage, the *News of the World* published a relatively unaggressive exposé, and there was no reason why this should have had any lasting impact on Robin Cook's career. But he was already developing difficulties with policy.

As those difficulties grew, so his Mission Statement began to mock him. Among its unexceptional sentiments was this sentence: 'Our foreign policy must have an ethical dimension and must support the demands of other people to the democratic rights on which we insist for ourselves.' There is nothing in that phrase to which any reasonable person – any recent Foreign Secretary – could object. Would anyone have a foreign policy without an ethical dimension, telling others they cannot have democratic rights? The point is tone. The Mission Statement was meant to be taken not as a quiet summary of consensual sentiments, but as a bold declaration, and so it was, in particular by Labour MPs who thought it unethical to supply weapons to dictators. Those MPs included Robin Cook. He had made this plain in Opposition, from a long way back. But he found himself unable to stop a contract signed by the previous government to supply Hawk jets to the oppressive regime then in control of Indonesia. The legal advice on revoking licences was discouraging, the likely compensation prohibitive, and the Prime Minister in favour of upholding the contract. The decision to let the remaining sales go ahead was a grave disappointment to precisely the kind of MPs who were Robin Cook's admirers in the Labour Party: bad enough in any case, but very damaging in its contrast with the high-minded tone of the Mission Statement. The argument over Hawk jets was part of a wider tussle with Number Ten over criteria for arms sales. Alastair Campbell described the Foreign Secretary's proposals as 'pure leftism' [diary 23 July 1997]. Long after Labour left behind unilateralism and withdrawal from the Common Market, issues like arms sales remained divisive. For Tony Blair the question was primarily about jobs at huge exporters like British Aerospace. Robin Cook learned a swift and brutal lesson in the limits of power, even in one of the supposed great offices of state, as the Prime Minister's team watered down his arms criteria.

To have set the word 'ethical' as the criterion by which every move will be measured was inviting harsh judgements: and in they came.

Robin Cook's reputation for competence was damaged by a controversy during a Royal visit when India reacted contemptuously to an apparent offer by the Foreign Secretary of British mediation in Kashmir. The damage was not so much that he had offended India as that, far worse for the media, he had embarrassed the Queen.

The Foreign Secretary was pilloried for upsetting the

Israeli Prime Minister, Binyamin Netanyahu, by criticising his policy of building settlements. Robin Cook chose to make his point during a visit to what was then a new Israeli settlement between Bethlehem and Jerusalem, called Har Homa. It has become one of the most important, described by the Israeli Prime Minister in March 2015 as 'a way of stopping Bethlehem from moving toward Jerusalem.'

So the decision to draw attention to Har Homa in 1998 was right from the point of view of Britain's policy, then and now, of opposing the building of Jewish towns on land where a Palestinian state would be, under a two-state solution. But principled policy was lost amid tactical misjudgements about how and where to make a serious point: one of the keys to successful foreign policy. The *New York Times* described the visit as 'brief, tumultuous and soggy', reporting: '...pandemonium broke out, as Israeli militants and television crews mobbed Mr. Cook and a rainstorm erupted over them all. Whether by design or because they were caught by surprise, Israeli security men failed to hold back the demonstrators, who beat on pots and pans and screamed insults at Mr. Cook.... Soon after, Mr. Netanyahu's office announced that dinner was off, saying: ''The Prime Minister's meeting with the British Foreign Secretary will be shorter than planned. The Prime Minister decided not to hold a dinner with the British Secretary.'''

On the scale of diplomatic insults, a cancelled dinner ranks high. The British media did not applaud the Foreign Secretary for making a difficult policy clear, but ridiculed him for being stood up. When I started working at the Foreign Office, there was a cartoon on the FCO newsroom wall of the Foreign Secretary boarding his plane at Tel Aviv, turning to wave to no-one and saying: 'Er...well..... I'll be off then.' Ridicule can do more damage than heavyweight criticism.

Once a minister is going down, the media sees all he does as evidence of failure. I took part in this hunting pack many times as a political correspondent. There is no point offering the newsdesk a story about someone doing something good when he is obviously on the way down. You are looking for the next mistake, and if no mistake, no story. So newspapers which might otherwise have approved some honesty about an Israeli policy which they otherwise condemn, chose to highlight the supposed humiliation of being 'snubbed': a favourite word for reporters covering ministers perceived to have lost authority. Robin Cook might have been praised for taking an 'ethical' position at risk of Israeli anger, but that would have gone against the narrative. The media likes its narrative to be uncluttered: Robin Cook was in trouble and his ethical foreign policy to be ridiculed. Pictures of him being jostled in the rain at an Israeli settlement fitted the story. Nobody looks dignified beneath an umbrella failing to do its job. When a Foreign Secretary loses his dignity, his authority is washed away too, and with it the self-confidence necessary to fill a major job. It was especially enjoyable – nothing personal – for the media to see credibility draining from someone who had brought others down with his scintillating scorn.

And then there was the Sandline controversy, in which it seemed that the Foreign Office had connived at the breaking of a United Nations arms embargo in Sierra Leone, where Britain supported the democratically elected President Kabbah against a particularly violent rebellion. The damaging question was whether British support had violated international law, and around this question was a tangle of poorly-handled incidents that raised suspicions of ministers not keeping parliament properly informed. There were echoes of the Scott inquiry. As the columnist Donald

Macintyre wrote in *The Independent*: '....while officials now turn out to have been a good deal more reticent than they should have been, did Robin Cook really have to make a drama out of a crisis by reacting at the outset of the affair as if not he, but possibly his department, could be embroiled in the sort of re-run of the Scott affair that this certainly wasn't? Cook is probably the cleverest man in the Cabinet.... There is nevertheless a mounting sense, compounded by the harassment Cook faces over the business Britain does with the brutal regime in Indonesia, that not all is well in the department he is responsible for running.... relations between officials and ministers have been – at least temporarily – brought to a new low by an affair that should never have been allowed to run out of control as it has.'

In particular, relations between Robin Cook and Sir John Kerr, the Permanent Secretary of the Foreign Office – its chief civil servant – suffered irreparable damage. Neither of these spiky individuals, rightly proud of their brainpower but perhaps too aggressively intelligent, ever recovered confidence in the other. Both took personally the public humiliations the Foreign Office suffered while writhing uncomfortably with the display of incompetence provided by parliamentary inquiries into Sandline. The hostility between them was a lasting problem, diminishing both men, depriving their working relationship of the trust between ministers and officials that is essential at this level of government, shattering morale and weakening the Foreign office's performance for a long time. I was to witness this failed relationship close up for three years, and to grapple with its consequences throughout their remaining time of being yoked unhappily together in office.

The poor handling of Sandline – more than the substance of the affair – damaged what had been Robin Cook's greatest asset as Tony Blair formed his first government, his competence. He had played a large part in earning Labour the reputation for competence that a potential government must have, and now he was presiding over the sort of incompetence that no government can afford to become associated with. Competence in government is about the appearance as well as the substance, being seen to handle difficulties well, and to convey a sense of grip.

Alastair Campbell noted on successive days:

> *'RC was not responding well... TB called and asked why we were being so pathetic about it...'* [AC diary 8 May]

> *'Sandline was a growing problem and RC was getting totally into the bunker on it... It was one of those stories that the media got excited about but had very little real substance or problem to it, provided we were robust and saw it off... the differences between him and his officials were beginning to seep out.'* [9 May]

> *'TB was livid at the way Robin had handled it, and allowed a problem to become something worse. 'He had lost whatever – he ever had...'* [10 May]

> *'...the problem of course flowed from Robin's bloody ethical foreign policy statement after the election, which set him up for criticism at the slightest hint of trouble.'* [11 May]

Three
After the Fall

I was on a train pulling into Kings Cross station when my phone rang: 'This is the Foreign Secretary's office. Can you come in this afternoon?'

I was not surprised, because Alastair Campbell had taken me aside at a Number Ten party about a month before and asked if I was interested in 'helping Robin'. I was, as actors say, between engagements, having resigned from Piers Morgan's *Daily Mirror*. Nothing had happened since, except that Robin's need for help spiralled. That was painfully obvious to an outsider, though I didn't know until the publication of the Campbell diaries how appalled the Prime Minister had been, and that the night before the Foreign Office rang me, Alastair had recorded in his diary:

> *'RC called, claiming he was being briefed against. He was going to hire John Williams as Number 2 in the news department, and start to fight back a bit.' (May 7)*

I was shown up to the Ambassadors' waiting room where, allegedly, Ribbentrop was made to wait in 1939 to be told Britain and Germany were at war. (I never checked whether this was truth or the kind of intimidating myth that the Foreign Office likes). In came an old friend, John Grant, whom I had known as a brilliant young press officer during my *Evening Standard* days. He was now Robin's Principal Private Secretary, that is, the person who runs the Foreign Secretary's office. He looked pleased to see me, and over the next few months of working with John on one problem after another, I could see why he was so pleased to have someone new to help him. It had never occurred to me as a journalist that when a minister is in serious difficulty, it can be hell for the officials around him. John took me into the Foreign Secretary's room, which someone once said is big enough for three double decker buses. (I'd say that's an under-estimate.) John left me alone with Robin, sitting in a red leather chair at his desk. We were to have many such sessions, just the two of us mulling things over. I hadn't the slightest doubt that Friday afternoon that I was going to say yes. I wanted to work in government. And I actually wanted to take on the Foreign Secretary's problem, though I'm glad I didn't know quite the depth of despair in Number Ten at the way Robin Cook was coping with Sandline. He described the problem in outline and said it was serious, but he did not think terminal.

I was taken downstairs to see the Permanent Secretary, Sir John Kerr, again alone, who told me the Foreign Secretary couldn't be effective with the media on his back all the time, so my job would be to get them off. Oddly I was not taken to see the head of news, Nigel Sheinwald. He can't have been pleased at an outsider being brought in, but Nigel treated me with helpfulness and respect during the two or three months we worked together: he was due for promotion to be Director Europe within a few weeks [and as Sir Nigel Sheinwald would become UK Representative – ambassador – to the European Union, then chief foreign policy advisor to the Prime Minister, and finally UK Ambassador to

Washington]. I was filling the job of his deputy, Peter Bean, who had just died of a heart attack. I knew Peter very well and was extremely fond of him. It was terrible that his death was the reason for the vacancy.

It was agreed that I would start work in a week's time, during which there would be security checks and other working arrangements put in place. Over the weekend I heard on the news that Robin had cancelled all engagements to deal with Sandline. I was appalled. It seemed to me a disastrous signal of panic. I did wonder if the Foreign Secretary would still be there when I arrived.

When I did, he asked: 'Am I finished? And no bullshit.'

I said no. While I believe in honesty in all dealings, you can be just too brutal, and I judged that the Foreign Secretary didn't need a new advisor telling him what he must know, that his position was extremely precarious. This was my first instinctive grasping of the importance of raising morale in the role of the media advisor. My impression was that Robin and his team had come to a point at which it seemed anything they did might be the next mistake. Competence and confidence are close relatives: when they drift apart, it becomes impossible to cope under the kind of scrutiny that Cabinet ministers rightly work under. My advice was to take no media initiatives at all, on anything – disappear for a while – since the media can handle only one idea about anyone at one time, and for now, the idea attached to Robin was that he made mistakes. On that first day, May 17, a parliamentary question was answered with a genuine mistake about the number of meetings that had taken place on some aspect of Sierra Leone policy, which I had to go and correct on a walk around the press gallery, sensing Robin's credibility leaking like a punctured tyre. The answer which I was correcting must have been answered dishonestly or incompetently, in the media's perfectly reasonable view. Actually, it had been answered hastily. My first lesson was to insist thereafter on thorough checking of facts, even if the price was responding slowly. My second was that facts can be surprisingly hard to check, not because people are dishonest, though under pressure some are understandably reluctant to admit even to themselves precisely what happened. Even when they are established, the same facts can look very different to various people. In this case the facts were tangled and ambiguous, relating to a military coup against an elected government which then regained control, possibly with the help of British mercenaries (Sandline), perhaps authorised by the Foreign Office though maybe not.

The Prime Minister was exasperated that the Foreign Secretary was not boiling this down to the simple point that Britain had helped a democratic leader regain control after a bloodthirsty coup by some seriously unpleasant people. This was very Blair. He was brilliant at cutting through complexity and liked moral certainties. In many circumstances, this temperament was a strength. Things are not always quite that simple though.

By now, Robin didn't have the option of swatting aside the complexities, because he was entangled in them. They mattered, and if he had taken the Blair line that they didn't, he would have sounded both desperate and unconvincing. If it was true that in pursuing the good objective of helping President Kabbah fight off the rebels, Britain had connived at the breaking of a UN arms embargo, that couldn't be lightly dismissed. You can't do that. If you believe in international law based on morality, then you have to believe in it at all times, not dismiss it as a detail when it proves inconvenient. That is not 'ethical' but practical foreign policy, because to pick and choose your moments for obeying or ignoring the rule of law is to set yourself up for impossible dilemmas in the real world, not in the realm of idealism.

The hard problem we had, in Robin's team, at that moment, was that it wasn't clear precisely what had been done by whom. You can't take an ethical or moral stance when you don't know what the heck has happened.

I had a meeting with Alastair Campbell, whose advice was simple: 'Get a grip.' He didn't try to micro-manage me, though I had no experience in government nor as any kind of spokesman whatever. We knew each other pretty well, as journalists (I had succeeded Alastair as Political Editor of the *Mirror*). And he had plenty else to grapple with across the whole of government. He just wanted the problem to go away. So did Robin Cook, of course. He held a team meeting on a rainy Bank Holiday Monday at which I advised him to forget about the media – stop reading it – and let me deal with the newspapers while he got on with being Foreign Secretary. Nigel Sheinwald was his press secretary, travelling with him, while I got on with getting a grip at home. This was a good arrangement. Robin had to keep functioning as Foreign Secretary – no more cancelling engagements to deal with Sandline – while someone took the problem apart and decided how to deal with it.

It took a lot of time and work to establish what had and – as important – had not happened. The Foreign Office appointed a thorough young official called Rob Macaire to trace who had said what to whom on which day and at which meeting, and how decisions had been made or neglected. I went to see him in a small office stacked with all the relevant papers, and for several weeks we worked on the case like a pair of detectives. One of the main questions was where in the system a particularly important piece of paper had got stuck, since it clearly had not reached the Foreign Secretary.

This was a crash course for me in how government works, or fails to. My recollection is that we identified a long delay in a junior minister's box. It would not have been fair of Robin to shift the blame, and would have been fatal had he tried. My advice was to defend everyone and take the blame himself, however unjustly. This was hard advice, as the mistakes made had not been Robin's fault; nor even things that he could reasonably have been expected to know.

For example, on the central question of whether the FCO had authorised mercenaries to go into Sierra Leone in breach of a UN embargo, it seemed that the pivotal conversation had happened over lunch between the High Commissioner and the head of Sandline. Whether approval had been sought, given or done with a wink it was impossible to tell, as this was not properly reported up the line, and the Foreign Secretary found himself answering to parliament for it.

I was surprised that the Foreign Office could work in such a muddled way and thereafter went about the job sceptically, reluctant to take anything at face value. It would have taken the most uncanny curiosity on the part of the Foreign Secretary to have divined that people were lunching with mercenaries in a London restaurant, discussing intervention in an African state, apparently in pursuit of an ethical dimension to foreign policy. Given my vague job description – get a grip – I took a relentless curiosity to be a core task from then on.

The Foreign Secretary had three special advisors, David Clark, Andrew Hood and David Mathieson, all of whom were authorised to talk to the media. This political team and I worked well together, all agreed on the short-term tactic of going quiet, keeping things tight, while waiting for the media to get bored with Robin's troubles and move along to someone else. Nigel Sheinwald was succeeded by

Kim Darroch, who was also destined to become Director Europe and, as Sir Kim, to follow the same career trajectory through Brussels, the PM's Office, and Washington, as well as being UK National Security Advisor. The Foreign Office tradition was for the head of news to be a middle-ranking high-flier, rather than a specialist in dealing with the media: like Christopher Meyer, who had done a classy job for Sir Geoffrey Howe and finished up as Ambassador to Washington (as Sir Christopher). They had never had an outsider, from the media.

The most important working relationship was with the Foreign Secretary's private office. John Grant [later Sir John, UK Representative to the European Union] and his team – Andrew Patrick and Dominick Chilcott, followed by Tim Barrow – took to calling me The Grim Williams for always coming in with bad news. The point was to come in with it before it broke in the newspapers, preferably at a stage when we could prevent it happening.

The working method of a Cabinet Minister's office is that senior officials submit papers for decision through the principal private secretary, who schedules – in this case – the Foreign Secretary's meetings with policy officials, with fellow ministers, with the media and with visiting foreign ministers, plus his travel abroad. The role is more fundamental than timetabling, it is about the Foreign Secretary's priorities, and therefore to some extent Britain's priorities. There are every day far more issues of pressing concern than the Foreign Secretary can deal with: if he tries to concentrate on everything, he concentrates on nothing. He and his private office have to clear away the clutter of incoming telegrams and policy papers and media reports, and focus on what matters – all of them subjective judgements. An efficient minister knows by good instincts and hard work what matters enough to take on actively himself, what to note and put to one side for now, and what can probably be allowed to go by. He makes those judgements in formal meetings and in snatches of conversation while hurrying to his car or into Cabinet. And he makes them in what must be the loneliest part of the job, at the tired end of a long working day, when he takes from his pocket the key to his red box. Inside is a pile of paper, sifted skilfully by the principal private secretary, to put the most urgent decision-making papers at the top, but also to make sure that longer-term policy that will become very tough is not neglected at the bottom. The Foreign Secretary makes notes in the margins in red ink – red, so that everyone can see at a glance that it's from 'the boss' – in the form of questions, comments and decisions. (I don't know whether this very good old fashioned method has been superseded by email).

On a different scale, I would as press secretary face a similar mountain of papers, always with the feeling that all of it had to be read with an eye for the detail that might be the clue to the next big problem. It is an engrossing and, at its best, rewarding exercise, but there is always the knowledge that in this pile of paper may lurk the mistake you will always regret.

My pile of reading would be different from the Foreign Secretary's, because I would be seeing draft policy papers on their way up to him, for my comment. When a policy official writes a paper for the Foreign Secretary, he or she puts at the top a circulation list of all those whose views, consent or objections must be sought. If I disagreed or had an uneasy premonition, I would ask for a meeting of officials and special advisors, and test my instincts against theirs, usually collaboratively, though at times with some friction as a cherished piece of policy hit the hard instincts of the media advisor who will have to explain it publicly. The Foreign Secretary sees the outcome of those inter- actions between the professionals working for him, set out as analysis and recommendations, with some points about public presentation.

But not all decisions are made in that orderly fashion, nor are all problems detected by formal process. The Foreign Office was – and presumably still is – a humming hive of speculative, forward looking, in-house chatter and disputation and opinion-seeking about all the world's difficulties. It is the job of the Foreign Secretary's closest advisors – private office, special advisors, press secretary – to make themselves part of that running conversation, to hear the off-note in the orchestra that is the alert to something starting to go wrong, or switching metaphors, to sense a change in the weather.

Some officials, then and later, felt I was exaggerating problems, which I always took as an unintended compliment: you must be well on top of your problems if they seem exaggerated. This was not a view taken by all. John Grant and I struck a very close working relationship as joint bearers of bad tidings and fellow seekers after solutions to intractable problems. We both knew the Foreign Secretary had to get through the parliamentary inquiries into Sandline before any thought could be given to how he might recover his standing; or the Foreign Office, since its lofty reputation had come down in the world as its untidy handling of Sandline was minutely examined in sometimes painful select committee hearings, which we prepared for intensely. John Kerr had said something that contradicted the Foreign Secretary in one hearing, so from then on I conducted merciless grillings of officials before they appeared, to help them prepare, and to help me continue to work out exactly what had gone on. The point was to get the story straight, admit what fault there was, and stop digging holes. Once a problem goes past a certain point, the only way out is to admit fault gracefully and shut up.

Even when Rob Macaire's inquiries had provided assurance that in this bungled episode there was nothing the Foreign Secretary could be directly blamed for, publication of inquiry reports would be further festivals of ridicule for Ethical Foreign Policy. And there would be wide scope for mis-reaction. Ministerial careers are often ended by poor reactions to a problem rather than by the original problem. John Grant and I agreed with Robin that whatever the merits of the case, he would stick to defending officials. Some did deserve to be defended, but not all. One lesson of this episode for me was that the Foreign Office was unexpectedly mixed in the calibre of its staff: superb people jumbled with mediocre or worse at all levels. There is a difference between fine brains and sound judgement, being clever and being reliable. John Grant was at the top end of the range, on brains and judgement, and our close working relationship at this desperate time was invaluable, personally and professionally. Pressure can't be handled alone and we supported one another, as friends as well as professionals, both intrigued and perplexed – fascinated – by the challenge of pulling the Foreign Secretary and the Foreign Office through crisis.

The Foreign Secretary had appointed a QC, Sir Thomas Legge, to inquire into the Sandline fiasco. When his report was published on 27 July, and Robin Cook dutifully defended officials, this small but intensely damaging drama seemed to be over, though his problems were not. Even if they had been, it is unusual for a politician at that level to recover once so badly damaged. Neither Robin Cook nor the Foreign Office was likely to get any credit for whatever good work they did for some time, it seemed to me, but recovery could begin with some patiently competent work and more attention to potential menace from the media. One reason why the Foreign Office had got into difficulties was a tendency – not shared by all – to regard the media as not even a nuisance: not worth taking seriously, since it was so ill-informed and unreasonable that you couldn't do anything about it. Robin had gone on the Royal visit to India and Pakistan in 1997 without a press officer to deal with the tempest that suddenly raged over Kashmir, because the tradition was that a press officer was not required on such visits. It was time to do away with some traditions and deal with life as it now was. John Kerr had been right that a Foreign Secretary – any minister – cannot be effective while under media siege.

The next Royal visit was approaching, to Brunei and Malaysia. It was agreed with Buckingham Palace that I would go with Robin and Gaynor Cook as travelling press officer. They were now married, and there was bound to be some bloodsport for the Royal correspondents if they could get at the Foreign Secretary and his wife. The Queen's press secretary, Geoff Crawford, saw that a press officer was needed to keep them out of the news, not promote them into it. People were getting used to the idea that I saw my job as the opposite of the common conception of a press officer: no news, thanks. Sooner or later, Robin would be able to re-surface as a serious Foreign Secretary, if he had a long quarantine out of the headlines, I felt.

As well as accompanying the Foreign Secretary, I went out a couple of weeks in advance to 'recce' the visit. It seemed not to have occurred to the Foreign Office to recce difficult media terrain before, otherwise the Foreign Secretary's difficulties in Israel would not have been compounded by his humiliating photocall at Har Homa, as

42

anyone would have known by going in advance to walk the course with an eye – or a nose – for trouble. This incident had been a case study in the new harshness of a changing media, which not only lacked the old deference, but found it easier to report difficult encounters in terms of 'snubs' (a great word for short headlines) than by explaining the complexities involved. There was – is – no point deploring the superficiality, it has to be anticipated and a way found past it, by taking the trouble to explain and stage things well. In that case, it should have been obvious that the media would enjoy Israel's Prime Minister, Binyamin Netanyahu, making a spectacle of the Foreign Secretary by standing him up. John Grant and I were determined not to let anything like it happen again. The Foreign Secretary was in too weak a political condition.

John said: 'Go out there and put your nose to the ground'. I walked every step that the Queen and Foreign Secretary would take, so that I knew all the camera angles. More important I asked questions about the political situation, and sniffed the air. I picked up a scent of trouble in Malaysia, where the Prime Minister was at odds with his deputy. I asked what would happen – how bad would be the public order consequences? – if Mahatir Mohammed moved against Anwar Ibrahim while the Queen was in town. He won't, I was told. But what if? Don't worry, he won't while the Queen is here. As Mahatir's human rights record was not perfect, there was obvious scope for difficulty if trouble happened and the Queen's presence – on Foreign Office advice – was taken by the media as condoning his actions. This was the problem I sniffed with my nose to the ground.

Travelling with the Queen was a great pleasure. She likes to know everyone in the party, and is herself a consummate professional. She understood why the Grim Williams had been added to the usual cast of aides de camps, private secretaries, batmen and ladies in waiting.

Waiting for us was the rat pack, as the Royal correspondents were known. I knew some of them well from my years on the London *Evening Standard* and the *Daily Mirror;* in the case of Charlie Rae from *The Sun*, going back 20 years to our days as local industrial correspondents in Birmingham covering strikes at British Leyland. The rat pack was capable of making life hell, more than anyone in the British media. They all knew why I was there and we faced each other with relish. They weren't going to get anywhere near Gaynor.

This was stretching my job description as given by John Kerr, to keep the media off the Foreign Secretary's back, but Robin could not be taken seriously if the media turned him and his wife into a soap opera. Robin was preparing for one of his first serious achievements as Foreign Secretary, leaving the Royal visit a couple of days early to go to New York for the first ministerial meeting between Britain and Iran since the author Salam Rushdie had been condemned to death by Iran, and who had been living in hiding under close protection. This was to be the beginning of a delicate process which would involve an Iranian statement enabling Rushdie to emerge and resume a normal life. Exploring the potential to engage with an apparently less hardline Iranian regime would be the kind of serious work that a Foreign Secretary should be getting media coverage for, an opportunity for him and the Foreign Office itself to leave ridicule behind.

So the rat pack was not going to catch him out or make a media spectacle of his wife. The ladies in waiting were very helpful, always forming a bodyguard of large hats and swishing skirts around Gaynor, while Robin discreetly followed the floor plan of every site, which I had done so that the Cooks could keep discreetly in the background. My old friends in the rat pack soon lost interest, with grins of acknowledgement that they had been checkmated.

We were taking a break in Brunei – the Queen paces herself very sensibly – when John Grant took a call from Malaysia, where we were about to go next. Mahatir had sacked Anwar and people were protesting in the streets to the sound of gunfire. There wasn't any serious danger on security grounds, but there was politically. John and I sat down with Geoff Crawford and one of the Queen's private secretaries, Mary Francis, to discuss what to do. I said the Foreign Secretary must stay on the visit, rather than leave early for New York. He would seem to be leaving the Queen in difficulty, and the Foreign Office would be open to criticism for letting her get on with it, having recommended a visit at an unstable moment. Whether or not that would be fair, it would be how the newspapers would see it. I wasn't guessing. It's what I would have written had I still been on the other side on the barriers with my old friend Charlie Rae. It was agreed that Robin would delay his visit to New York and re-arrange his meetings with Iran. We mustn't make any great announcement about this, just let the rat pack know Robin was staying, as if nothing could be more obvious. This came out well, Robin portrayed as gallantly standing beside the Queen as she bravely went ahead.

The only problem with extending the Cooks' presence in the Royal party was that Gaynor didn't have enough hats and outfits: one can't appear twice in the same, alongside ladies in waiting who travel with enormous wardrobes. (I was enjoying the free laundry service provided by Royal batmen, who took very seriously their duty to ensure that the whole party emerged from the plane or from each hotel stop without a crease). I volunteered to take Gaynor shopping as soon as we arrived in Kuala Lumpur. As it happened, my brother-in-law Stephen was working there, and his wife Trudi was very happy to take the Foreign Secretary's wife – and a protection officer – to the best shops. This was by now a long way from foreign policy or any conventional idea of a press officer's role. But the job was done: there were no problems, and Robin was free to go to New York a couple of days late to join the head of news, Kim Darroch, for what the Foreign Secretary liked to call 'some serious diplomacy'. I went home with the Queen's thanks and a signed picture. This nice gesture caused some amusement to friends and family who knew me for a lifelong republican.

Robin was beginning to re-establish himself. He was working on another delicate piece of diplomacy, persuading Libya to hand over suspects for the Lockerbie bombing for trial in a third country. This was a clever idea conceived with the US Secretary of State, Madeline Albright. The Libyans were not prepared to hand suspects to Britain. Holland agreed to host a trial. As with Iran, this meant engaging with a regime, Gaddafi's Libya, that had a poor human rights record, in pursuit of a specific and just outcome. The word 'ethical' was not mentioned. I had advised against the temptation to re-launch or re-brand Robin Cook's foreign policy, but rather to get on with doing it until a point at which there was enough substance to put his early difficulties in perspective.

He had still not quite left his problems behind. His ex-wife Margaret had signed a publishing deal. Her book was going to be serialised in *The Sunday Times* in January 1999. This is how I described that episode in a note written after it was over:

'Robin, after some persuading, agreed to say
nothing and try to come through on a policy of
virtuous non-reaction. He could not afford anything
like the disastrous counter-offensive against his ex-
diary secretary when she had talked to the *Mirror*
in early 1998. To do anything like that against his
ex-wife would be suicidal.'

I am referring here to one of Robin's misjudgements when
his troubles began soon after becoming Foreign Secretary.
He had tried to bring in Gaynor as his diary secretary, and
when attacked for doing so he had spoken critically of the
incumbent: an example of poor public reaction compounding
a relatively minor problem. It was clear to me that if he or
anyone associated with him spoke critically of his ex-wife,
it would reflect very badly on him, perhaps fatally. Taking
criticism quietly goes against all the instincts and working
methods of politicians and their advisors. Alastair Campbell
had brought in a culture of 'rebuttal' – the jargon word of
the trade of media communication – which meant quick,
often aggressive responses to anything critical in the media.
This is standard technique in the trade, and it is often a
necessary means of challenging inaccurate or misleading
media reports. Untruths and misperceptions can become
facts if unchallenged. There is no reason why politicians
should allow that. They are entitled to defend themselves,
sometimes loudly. But as a newcomer to the trade I took a
slightly different approach, that there was value in turning
the volume down, tolerating legitimate criticism and at
times letting hurtful attacks go unanswered. Rebuttal can be
desperately undignified; constant complaining phone calls to
journalists self-defeating; and some problems made worse
by protesting too much. Robin Cook accepted my personally

painful advice that he would have to sit out his ex-wife's book in silence, as I noted:

'The real problem was not Robin, who agreed to be silent, but the sources close to him. It was hard to see a way of preventing the papers getting them to react.

With his approval, over Christmas, I told Phil Webster [political editor of *The Times*] that Robin was telling all his 'friends' and 'sources close to' that they were to take a vow of silence. Phil's Boxing Day page lead put everyone on notice, and let the media know to expect no reaction. Of course, it wasn't going to be quite as simple as that, but we had set the right expectations, and it worked.

The *Sunday Times* was due to begin serialisation on January 10. The week before, Robin rang selected editors to tell them he wasn't going to react. On the Friday and Saturday, I spent hours on the phone to all the Sundays; partly to find out what they were hearing (big exclusives usually leak from newsroom to newsroom) and partly to get them used to the idea that I was the one dealing with this, not any of the friends and sources.

Early on the Saturday evening, around 7pm, Tom Baldwin [then the political editor of the *Sunday Telegraph* and later stretgy advisor to Ed Miliband as Leader of the Opposition] rang to say he was hearing that Margaret Cook was saying Robin was a drunk.

I rang Robin at Chevening to tell him the worst. It was not an easy thing to say, but his only reaction was professional – what do you plan to do? I said

I thought we had to deal with the drink problem.
The lobby knows who the drunks are and Robin
had never been one of them. I would get that over,
speaking to the lobby as 'a friend authorised to
speak on Robin Cook's behalf'. That way, they
would know there was only one source of comment
on this and that source was restricted to commenting
on one allegation which they knew to be wrong.'

Robin Cook had attracted loyalty as well as jealousy during
his Commons career and I had offers of help from colleagues
who wanted to defend him, in the days leading up to
publication. Harriet Harman, then Social Services Secretary,
and Frank Dobson, Health Secretary, both wanted to speak
up for him, but Robin asked them to consult me.

'Frank did a typically robust defence on Sunday
lunchtime radio, though without criticising
Margaret Cook, when I felt there needed to be one
friendly voice on the airwaves. All the friends and
sources close to Robin acted with the agreed self-
discipline, despite heavy pressure from reporters to
say something critical of the book.

Harriet had been Robin's deputy during the
period Margaret was writing about and, by luck, I
had run into her the week before – she had said, if
there's anything I can do, call me.

By now, the *Sunday Times* story was all round
Fleet Street. For the rest of that weekend and the
next, I had both home phones and the mobile
ringing almost constantly. While fielding calls,
I asked Pam [my wife] to get the Number Ten
switchboard to raise Harriet. When Harriet came

on, I read to her a statement I proposed to use in her name – to the effect that she worked all hours with Robin at the time and never saw him drinking. So, for that night, I was both Harriet Harman and a friend of Robin Cook.

This went on till midnight, including negotiations with Alastair over whether Tony Blair should or shouldn't comment on the Frost programme next morning. Prime Ministerial support can cut either way with the media, but we and Robin all felt it had to be done.

We had an appalling media, of course. It was too lurid a story not to get technicolour coverage, but it wasn't hostile. That may sound silly. But I had always felt that the crucial question was whether this was reported because it was a damn good story, or because it gave them a chance to go for the kill. When I say it wasn't hostile, I mean they weren't going for the kill. The moment when I felt we were going to come through was when Trevor Kavanagh [political editor of *The Sun*] said – he'll be OK, there's nothing here to finish him off. *The Sun's* coverage was horribly cruel – a 'would you sleep with this man?' phone-in – but they were treating it as a joke.'

We had set up 'some serious diplomacy', for Robin to be getting on with in spite of his wife's book: the point being to show that it wasn't going to affect him as Foreign Secretary. Robin was interested in engaging more deeply with Russia and its foreign minister, Igor Ivanov, so I recommended a visit. Robin's forging of strong relationships with fellow foreign ministers – Albright, Ivanov and Hubert Vedrine of France especially – was beginning to be noticed by the media.

John Grant suggested that I go to Russia and do a recce. We both had in mind something more than the usual visit – in and out for talks at the foreign ministry – instead taking a media party out into the country to signal the importance of a stronger partnership. And we would need some policy announcement, something Britain would offer to do to help Russia in its long journey away from the recent history of dictatorship. The embassy arranged a programme of meetings for me in Ekaterinberg, where the governor offered to host the Foreign Secretary at his dacha, and St Petersberg, astonishingly beautiful under fresh snow, with opportunities for some sort of cultural partnership. But we found what we were looking for in Murmansk, where former Soviet nuclear submarines were sitting in the harbour going rusty, leaking pollution into the sea.

Robin liked the idea of a British fund to dismantle this terrifying legacy of the Cold War and opened negotiations with the Treasury. He was not so enamoured of the idea of visiting Murmansk in midwinter. He took out an atlas and checked that, yes, it was inside the Arctic Circle. I agreed that it was a bleak setting. It had been dark all day while I was up there, the temperature minus 20. I argued that Robin needed to be doing unglamorous things that had specific results, a serious man doing things that mattered. The unspoken message was – not making overblown speeches about ethical foreign policy; too big for the media to belittle, rising above his difficulties. He agreed, despite the temperature in the frozen north.

I wanted this visit done properly, with detailed attention to the way press conferences and pictures were set up: no repeats, ever again, of the humiliating pictures in Har Homa. I took to referring to Har Homa as shorthand for ill-prepared media work that held foreign policy up to ridicule. The

Foreign Office news department had never thought about properly organising something as fundamental to the business of projecting foreign policy as the Secretary of State's visits. In the good old days of deference, concentrating solely on the diplomacy had been correct and safe, but the balance between the policy and the presentation had to be shifted in an era of aggressively undeferential media scrutiny. What a Foreign Secretary says and does, where he says and does it, in what context, and on what timing, are crucial elements of foreign policy. In Har Homa, an ill-prepared event had resulted not in putting pressure on Israel to stop pre-empting the two-state solution with settlement building, but in pictures that made a fool of the Foreign Secretary.

I was able to get Murmask right – and every visit thereafter – thanks to the discovery that my secretary, Pat Barrie, had a flair for this kind of organisation, despite having no media background herself. She had replied to a Foreign Office advert while working for Liverpool Social Services and spent most of the last decade on postings in Greece and Uruguay, where she had run the ambassador's office. Back home, and after maternity leave, she saw an internal advert for PA to the Deputy Head of News and gave it a try. It was immediately clear she was resourceful and restless for responsibility, curious about the media and what this outsider from Fleet Street was up to all by himself in Room W1, across the corridor from the newsroom. She liked dealing with journalists and they liked her openness, telling them frankly when they weren't going to get an interview, but far more helpful with arrangements around press conferences and broadcast events than they were used to in dealing with Whitehall. Over the years – with Robin and then with Jack Straw – Pat's energy and creativity under pressure became the bedrock of an FCO media operation that was respected around the world for straight dealing. But at this stage she was as much a beginner to media work as I was to foreign policy. We both rebelled against the approach that, just because things had always been done a certain way, so they must continue to be; or that, just because something had never been done, it shouldn't be tried. Impossible was a banned word in Room W1.

Pat had already got a grip on my chaotic working schedule and on the flow of policy papers through my office, all of which had to be quickly read and mastered by a policy novice. Now she took charge of the travelling media party, never having done anything like it, working it out as she went along, making sure all the arrangements worked perfectly, all the press conferences were set up just right, and the pictures helped make the point rather than undermine it. The only thing missing when we arrived in Murmansk was the policy itself: the Treasury had still not agreed how much Robin could announce for dismantling nuclear submarines. Pat typed Robin's press conference statement with the figure missing, while the private secretary, Tim Barrow, conducted last minute negotiations on the phone, and Robin and I tried not to worry. Neither of us was very good at that. Just in time, Tim came off the phone, Pat typed in the missing number, and Robin went out to face the press.

The deepening friendship with Igor Ivanov was to be increasingly important as the Balkans slipped into conflict. Serbia's ethnic oppression in Kosovo was becoming worse. There was a shocking report one Saturday morning of murders in a place called Racak. The distinguished author on Balkan wars, Misha Glenny, reported in the *New York Times*:

*'The massacre last week in the Serbian province
of Kosovo followed a well-established pattern:*

Albanian guerrillas in the Kosovo Liberation Army kill a Serb policeman or two. Serb forces retaliate by flattening a village. This time they took the lives of more than 40 ethnic Albanians, including many elderly and one child..... The crucial question is, What are the motives of Yugoslavia's President, Slobodan Milosevic? There is little doubt that he approved the police action in Racak.'

Serbian responsibility for the killings was later disputed, but the impact at the time was a factor in moving international opinion against Serbia. I noted: 'This was the incident that made Robin determined that the Serbian leader, Slobodan Milosevic, had to be stopped.'

But the Foreign Secretary was still not free from his domestic political difficulties. Sandline returned to the headlines, and the problem was my fault. I had made a mistake. When a leaked copy of the Foreign Affairs Committee report showed up in Robin's office, I should have realised this was wrong and said it should be sent back wherever it came, without a glance. I read it and found it predictable from the tone and direction of questions during the committee hearings. As I didn't intend to react to the report in detail, but give the simple response that anyone criticised had Robin's full support, I put it in a drawer and didn't look at it again. And as the media was ringing up with questions which showed familiarity with the text, it didn't occur to me that it was one thing for newspapers and broadcasters to get leaks, another for government. I was caught out by a sudden controversy when the fact of our leak was leaked. It turned out to have come from a Labour backbencher close to Robin, Ernie Ross, who had thought he was being helpful. Robin wasn't prepared to shop Ernie as the leaker, and at one point said he would rather resign. I felt he meant it.

'We sat down one Monday morning – Robin, me, Andrew Hood [special advisor] – to decide whether the Margaret storm had passed. I said: 'There's another coming.'

This was a week ahead of the Foreign Affairs Committee report on Sandline. I'd had a leaked copy in my bottom drawer for a while, had read it, and noted that it was thoroughly predictable.

That morning I said to Robin that the only thing that mattered was for him to be seen to be backing officials. With his permission, I would keep playing that line to anyone who got a leak from the committee, as they did. I started getting calls on the Thursday, all the same – this will be very critical of officials, including Kerr. I said: 'If it's as you say, Robin will give full support.'

This isn't, to be honest, quite how he feels, but it's the only tenable position to take. And it worked. We killed the story in a matter of hours: perfect.

I was very careful not to use the leak, either to do pre-emptive leaking of my own, or even to base my replies on. I always said – if what you are being told is true....

It never occurred to me that we would be criticised for receiving a leak. But we were.

We spent several agonising days, including one harrowing Friday morning at 1CG [1 Carlton Gardens, the Foreign Secretary's official residence], waiting for Robin to resolve his dilemma. He seemed determined to protect Ernie [Ross] at any cost, including his own survival. The one alternative to the truth that he was prepared to consider was to stonewall and refuse to answer questions. We acknowledged that Robin was toying with a course of action that could quickly finish him, but we both knew he was right on the edge. Eventually he had a talk to Ernie, who saw that he was going to be exposed whatever happened – the Tory PQs [parliamentary questions] were too well targeted – and so he quit the committee and we gave straight, full answers. The story broke while we were in Moscow [during the visit to Russia mentioned earlier, in March 1999] . I was walking across Red Square with Pat, looking for somewhere to eat, when I got the first call. We had a couple of bad days, including a hard interview with John Humphrys, whose terms I negotiated as Robin waited, but it soon went away: only for the Standards and Privileges Committee to investigate.

It was an utterly bogus row. As a result, both Gordon Brown and Donald Dewar were forced to own up to soliciting select committee leaks.

What I blame myself for is not doing something improper – I was positively boy-scout-ish when you think what other spin doctors might have done – but that I failed to see how the mere receipt of the leak might damage us. I have made lots of little mistakes, as everyone does, but this was my one big error I hope.'

John Grant and I were summoned to a public hearing by the Commons Standards and Privileges Committee. John took this hard. He had been through a nightmare time before my arrival, and blamed himself harder than he should for the problem we now had. He was genuinely stricken that this should have happened just as it seemed the Foreign Secretary was putting his troubles behind him. In fact, this turned out to be the low point, and that John was going to be able to hand over to his successor, having made a huge contribution to Robin's recovery. In fact, I knew several members of the committee from my time as a political correspondent and sensed a worldly sympathy among them as they directed most of their questions at me, in a tone that made me think they did not see the leak as a political hanging offence. They knew other ministers had had similar tip-offs from friendly MPs on select committees.

And I felt the media no longer saw Robin as an endangered species. Wounding though his wife's serialisation had been for him personally, many journalists found it excessive and began to feel Robin had taken more punishment than was due. The editor of the Today Programme, then Rod Liddle, rang me and offered to interview Robin on any subject we liked, with a guarantee to ask nothing about his marriage.

So we were where I had wanted to be, with the media at last prepared to take Robin seriously as Foreign Secretary, not as the central character in a political farce.

Four
A Good War

The Foreign Secretary was heavily preoccupied with the worsening violence in Kosovo throughout 1998 and deeply involved in diplomacy to prevent it, followed by international co-ordination as NATO prepared for war in early 1999. The Balkans had been bloodily unstable for nearly a decade, since the break-up of Yugoslavia into half a dozen countries, letting loose ancient national and ethnic hatreds. The disintegration of Bosnia had led to racial mass murder on a scale that shocked Europe and left a legacy of guilt that little had been done to stop it. That conflict was not long resolved, when it became gruesomely clear that something similar was under way next door. Serbia was pursuing a policy of violent suppression of Kosovan autonomy, resulting in 1,500 deaths. Tony Blair, who had criticised his predecessor, John Major, for failing to intervene in Bosnia, told his Cabinet that Britain and its allies must now be prepared to use force if diplomacy could not halt the bloodshed.

Serbia regarded Kosovo as a province, and its actions there a sovereign matter. Kosovans rejected direct control by Serbia. NATO foreign ministers resolved in May 1998 to work for a peaceful solution and to safeguard the stability of neighbouring countries. In June NATO defence ministers decided to consider military options. The Foreign Secretary chaired a meeting of foreign ministers at Heathrow Airport on 6 October, which secured an understanding with Igor Ivanov that Russia would not intervene on the side of its ally Serbia if NATO took military action. Managing the relationship with Ivanov was one of Robin Cook's distinctive and at times difficult contributions to NATO's diplomacy.

NATO ordered air strikes to stop Serbian aggression on 13 October, but they were called off at the last minute when a NATO diplomatic mission persuaded the Serb leader, Slobodan Milosevic, to end the violence. This lasted only a few weeks. On 15 January, the bodies of more than 40 Kosovans were found in a gully in a village called Racak, an atrocity which made clear that Milosevic's military and police forces were undeterred by diplomacy. On 30 January 1998, NATO renewed its threat to use air strikes. France hosted a lengthy series of international negotiations in February and March, at the end of which Serbia refused to sign a proposed peace agreement, instead launching a new offensive. On March 23, NATO finally launched a campaign of air strikes.

The early days of the conflict were a disaster. Milosevic intensified the assault on Kosovo's civilian population, driving thousands across the border into Macedonia. Our media responded aggressively, taking the view that the agony of the refugees showed how misguided the NATO intervention was, and how inept the British and other governments had been not to foresee this. The military intervention was branded a failure before it had barely begun. A briefing by officials for Sunday newspapers resulted in headlines saying the Foreign Office had admitted 'failure'. In fact, the 'admission' was that it had been a 'failure of imagination' to get inside the head of someone like Milosevic, who was prepared to increase human suffering to put pressure on NATO. The British media was moving smartly into a default assumption that this was all going wrong. Thus the pressure increased on

NATO, as intended. This was the first of several times that I wondered how undemocratic people like Milosevic could know how to apply pressure on democratic leaders through their media.

Macedonia feared it was going to be overwhelmed by refugees. Robin persuaded its government to accept them during a long, agonising Saturday, ensuring that the UN could go in and help prevent a humanitarian catastrophe under a formula in which the refugee camps would be deemed UN territory, not Macedonian. We announced this the moment it was agreed: urgent as the humanitarian situation was, we needed to start turning our media opinion if we were to avoid a damaging loss of public consent.

In media terms, we were badly adrift. NATO's own press operation consisted of a fine spokesman, Jamie Shea, and no back office. Alastair Campbell went to Brussels to work out what help Jamie needed and reported that he was doing everything himself, writing his own press conferences and presenting them, while inundated with phone calls. Alastair organised a news operation for Jamie within a few days, seconding press officers from all over Europe. This was Alastair at his most energetic and decisive. One of his suggestions for co-ordinating the big NATO countries was a daily conference call involving spokesmen from Britain, France, Germany, Italy and the US: five countries known in diplomatic terms as 'the Quint'. I was our 'Quint' representative. Our conclusions were reported to Jamie Shea, so that he would now have a means of speaking on member countries' behalf, reflecting their positions, differences having been dealt with during our daily call. Each of the five spokespeople reported our conclusions – problems identified, solutions suggested, themes for statements and interviews etc – to our foreign ministers, who had their own

'Quint' call later each day. I would go up to private office to listen to their conference call, so that I knew what they were deciding and what was troubling them.

Meanwhile I suggested that to turn our own media and public opinion round, Robin and the Defence Secretary, George Robertson, should do a daily press conference – alternating – at 11.30 each morning. Jamie Shea would then pick up its theme at his daily 2.30pm press conference, and the US State Department spokesman would pick up the story at his daily briefing in late afternoon our time: all co-ordinated by Quint calls.

This meant that every other morning, I would go with Robin Cook and the relevant FCO officials to the Defence Secretary's morning briefing on the military action, taking reports from senior commanders. Robin and I would then go up to the MoD canteen for a fried breakfast to discuss what, from the briefing, he would say to the media at 11.30. He would go off to War Cabinet while I went to a room lent to me by the Chief of Defence Staff, General Sir Charles Guthrie. My secretary, Pat Barrie, would join me and I would dictate a press conference script to her, asking an MoD or FCO press officer to check facts, and relying on George Robertson's excellent private secretary, Tom McKane, to get any information needed. Robin and Charles Guthrie would come back, we would go through the script to add whatever had come out of War Cabinet, Pat would run it off, and then the four of us would get in the lift and go down to a press conference room packed with reporters for a briefing that was taken live throughout Europe and the United States. Guthrie was a wonderfully commanding presence alongside Robin, who thrived on the demands of explaining what was a moral – even ethical – intervention to prevent racial massacres. We never, ever used the word 'ethical'.

We decided to do a press conference with Igor Ivanov, the Russian foreign minister, as part of a visit to Robin's Edinburgh constituency. Relations with Russia were tense as the bombing continued, but remained good between the foreign ministers. I went up to Edinburgh to review arrangements and prepare, spending the evening before dictating the press conference script to Pat and then going out to dinner with her and the private secretary, Tim Barrow. Tim took a call: NATO had bombed the Chinese embassy in Belgrade.

First thing in the morning, Tim rang me and said Ivanov had cancelled his visit in protest. Robin was already booked for an interview on the Today programme.

'I hear we have a problem,' he said laconically, when I arrived at his flat, the radio car waiting in the rainy street.

'What do you suggest I say to John Humphrys?'

'Sorry. Make sure you apologise before he demands it.'

I soon found the effort of press conferences every other day hard to sustain, as there was precious little new information at the Defence Secretary's briefing, little evidence of progress in the military action. Often Pat would sit with her fingers ready over her keyboard and I had nothing to work with except words expressing good intentions. Somehow we always managed to put something together for when War Cabinet ended.

One morning our usual room was taken, so George Roberston said we could use his. I was still struggling when George breezed in, only to retreat, insisting that we finish. Robin's press conferences tended to emphasise the diplomacy more than the military action. Two eminent international figures were dispatched to go and see Milosevic: Victor Chernomyrdin and Marti Aatisaari. These were difficult names for Pat to get right over and over at speed as I dictated – usual spellings, I would say, as to newspaper copytakers in the old days of Fleet Street. You have to laugh at something under pressure. The morning they were due to fly to Belgrade, we felt the press conference script would be straightforward: Robin could spell out the message they were taking with them. It was a good script, of fine sentiments. The trouble was that just as Robin Cook and Charles Guthrie came in, Pat took a call that the Chernomyrdin-Aatisaari mission had been delayed. We weren't sure if they could go at all. That didn't leave Robin much to say.

He asked me to have a think about that while he went to the gents.

'What are you going to do?' said Pat, fingers poised over keyboard.

'I don't know. I'm just going to dictate until he comes back. Let's see what comes out. When he walks in, cut and paste, and pick up the script here...' pointing to a passage not related to Chernomyrdin-Aaatisari. We got away with it, because Robin was by now in command of the media, able to busk with authority when needed. US Congressmen told him that his and George Robertson's live press conferences, which came on during American breakfast television peak time, had done more than anything to steady opinion. Better, when Milosevic stopped the massacres and NATO's campaign succeeded, the Kosovan leaders came out of hiding and told Robin that those press conferences had kept them going because he couldn't possibly let them down after speaking so strongly day after day.

I recalled in my note at the end of the year:

> 'An account of Robin's 1999 has to give him credit for Kosovo. At the end of it, I said to him: 'You ought to stand back a minute and tell yourself that, whatever else happens in your career, you can

now be satisfied that you have done something worth doing, which wasn't easy to do. Not many politicians achieve that.'

What did he do? The arguments will never be settled – to what extent did NATO provoke or prevent the atrocities? What was our legal base?

To Robin, the issue was always simple and I was glad to get it down for him in plain language that helped us win – or at least avoid defeat – in the media war. We could not let a whole people be driven from a European country, under threat of death, on racial grounds, by state-sponsored violence. To all the legal, moral, military, diplomatic, geopolitical and human questions this conflict raised, the answer is that this could not be ignored. Milosevic would have slaughtered his victims at leisure and every death would have been on our conscience.

Robin showed himself to be one of those players who is at his best in the big games, under pressure, against the best opponents. I listened to some of his daily five-way phone conversations with his US, French, German and Italian counterparts and I have no doubt that his judgement and Albright's American clout dominated the fascinating, high stakes diplomatic game that 'The Quint' orchestrated. I remember one fairly heated debate, one evening, when Madeleine suddenly said: 'Hang on, hang on, I want to hear what Robin has to say about this.'

He drafted – with the help of top class officials like Emyr Jones Parry and Peter Ricketts – most of the key passages in the Security Council Resolution hammered out with Ivanov of Russia as the basis of the peace. [Emyr Jones Parry was Political Director, that is the most senior London-based official dealing with diplomatic negotiations, Peter Ricketts his Deputy. Sir Emyr was later UK Representative to the United Nations, Sir Peter was Ambassador to Paris and FCO Permanent Secretary].

After it was over, he was mobbed on the streets of Pristina. He rang me and said – listen to this.

When I told him I had kept a video of the jubilant crowd scenes, he said: 'Is that for me to watch when things go wrong in future?'

By the time Kosovo was relieved, the general journalistic view of Robin was that he was back as a big player. Tony Blair offered him the NATO secretary-generalship, not as a way of easing him out but because he was under pressure to provide a big British figure. Robin decided to stay in the Cabinet. Blair told him he's safe at the Foreign Office. [Defence Secretary George Robertson went to NATO.]

We hadn't got to this position by accident. The most important thing was his own competence and creativity. As well as Kosovo, he had crafted the compromise which induced Libya to hand over the Lockerbie suspects. It takes more than a good performance to convince the media, though. We had taken to having a group of columnists in to see him, we had had regular briefings for the Sundays and he had flogged himself round the studios, from Today to Larry King Live. And we had cut the frills: no personality interviews or profiles, just serious, solid work. He had avoided mistakes.'

Robin Cook's problems – the media indignities – were not forgotten. But it was clear now that he had been big enough to get a grip. The media was no longer looking only for chances to pounce on mistakes, but back in the old habit of respecting his qualities. He was a serious Foreign Secretary, having had a good war, in both senses, that Kosovo was military action in a good cause, and that Robin himself had given a good performance.

Five
The Hall of Mirrors

When the conflict was over, the future of the Balkans as a stable, democratic region became one of the Foreign Secretary's main preoccupations. On 30 July, 1999, he travelled with the Prime Minister to a conference chaired by President Clinton under the title The South East Europe Stability Pact. We flew to Banja Luka and then went by helicopter over glorious dream-country, wooded hills and deep gorges and vistas of distant blue mountains into Sarajevo sports stadium.

I noted a conversation with Alastair Campbell as we waited to brief British political correspondents, known as the lobby.

"I hate them, I really hate them."

"It's starting to show, Alastair."

"They're so stupid."

"Weren't you and I stupid when we were in the lobby?"

"No, we were far better than this lot."

"You're starting to sound very old, Alastair."

"They're nowhere near as good as we were. Even the older ones who were around in our day have become stupid. You look at Oakley and Brunson [Robin Oakley and Michael Brunson, political editors of the BBC and ITN]. They're not stupid, but they've been dragged downmarket by the papers."

The background to this outburst was the reshuffle. It was a very odd reshuffle, lots of speculation about Mo, Frank, Jack and Margaret [that is, Mowlam, Dobson, Straw, Beckett] and then, suddenly, no sackings, or moves, only Paul Murphy coming in to replace Alun Michael, who's off to lead the Welsh Assembly. Charles Reiss [political editor, *Evening Standard*] had told me he thought Alastair had wanted to make fools of the lobby. I found this implausible, but I wondered after that conversation in the bowels of the Zetra Olympic Stadium, Sarajevo.

Alastair said: "I told them over and over they were writing rubbish."'

It was a significant reshuffle for Robin Cook, because he acquired his long-standing supporter Peter Hain as Minister of State, with Geoff Hoon becoming Europe Minister. They were two of the brightest ministers one rung down from Cabinet, making the Foreign Office team exceptionally strong. Robin was less enthusiastic about Geoff's promotion than Peter's. He had not wanted to lose Joyce Quin as Europe Minister to make way for Geoff Hoon, whom Robin saw as uncomfortably close to Tony Blair. I wrote this a few days later, on 1 August 1999:

'On the morning of the reshuffle, Robin called me into his room. He was not happy. Though he had got his friend Peter Hain, he was upset at Joyce Quin's removal and peeved at getting John Battle as Tony Lloyd's replacement [as parliamentary under-secretary].

"I said I'd rather have someone off the backbenches. I would have put up more of a fight, but there wasn't much I could do, talking down a telephone to Tony from an airport runway in Estonia, with a band playing. I could kick myself for being out of the country."

He said the PM had told him he was replacing Joyce because he wants the job done with more oomph.

I said:"He means more media oomph."

While the Prime Minister appoints all members of the government, Cabinet ministers have some choice about the roles allotted to their Ministers of State and Parliamentary Under-Secretaries. The PM wanted Geoff Hoon switched from Minister of State for the Middle and Far East, to Europe, leaving Robin to decide which parts of the world the rest of the team would cover. This was a matter for discussion with the Permanent Secretary, Sir John Kerr, and the new Principal Private Secretary, Sherard Cowper-Coles, who had recently replaced John Grant. Running the Foreign Secretary's office is a demanding job usually held for no more than two years, at which point comes promotion to ambassador. John was rewarded with Sweden. Sherard had returned to London from a senior post in Paris. Sir Sherard would go on to be ambassador to Israel, Saudi Arabia and Afghanistan.

'Sherard came in with a huge Atlas, which Robin spread out. He was deciding what to give Peter Hain.

"I want to give him all this across here," Robin waved a hand over North Africa, the Middle and Far East. John Kerr came in and waited while

Robin and I agreed a media line.

I said:"We want Geoff Hoon seen as a boost for you and the Foreign Office, helping us to give Europe a push as our issue."

Robin winced.

"Not fair on Joyce, but I suppose we have no choice."

But in general, the Foreign Secretary was happy with the way things were going, at last. A note from 5 August, 1999:

'Robin said he wanted to see me on his last day in the office before the summer holiday. I was there when he came back from a long lunch with John Kerr.

'Come in, John.'

Sherard whispered: 'Don't take too long. Please don't take too long. We've so much to get through.'

Robin took off his jacket and kicked off his shoes. He has a way of sitting in the red chair at his desk, turned to one side with one leg draped over the chair arm. Does he only do that when feeling good? I'll have to check.

He had said he wanted to talk 'media strategy', but in fact he wanted a natter. I said I was unpopular in private office for taking his time and shouldn't take too much.

'Don't let them get to you.'

When I offered him another chance later to terminate the conversation, he said: 'I'm enjoying this. It's more fun than what they want me to do.'

There's a naughty boy in Robin that wants to put work off. He does the work though. There's been a hailstorm of private secretary minutes this week about an amazing diversity of things he has taken

an interest in or taken decisions on. I think much of
the FCO misreads his intensity. He's not prepared
to skim, so he doesn't tackle things until he's ready
to tackle them properly. That can be frustrating, but
it is surely a key to his quality. He's not prepared to
do anything less than well.'

This was my view, not impartial of course. Jonathan Powell,
an FCO official who became chief of staff to the Prime
Minister throughout the Blair years, writes in his book
on government that Robin Cook 'did not, however, apply
himself to the grind of governmental work and found a
lot of policy work boring. As a result, he never lived up to
his true potential as a Minister.' There were some Foreign
Office officials, especially dealing with the grind of Europe,
who took that view of Tony Blair. I felt, and still do, that
criticisms of workrate were cover for disapproval of policy,
as if the only explanation for a senior figure coming to
different conclusions to oneself must be lack of application.

By the summer of 1999, Robin Cook had come through
a long period of intense pressure, and had pulled through by
getting some difficult things right. He was entitled to bask,
just a little.

> 'He strolled about that ludicrously large office and
> said we'd done well this year, the two of us. We
> both groped about for wood to touch and I said we
> hadn't got to tempt, but yes – I don't believe there
> has ever been a politician of his size in as much
> trouble as he was in. I told him about a conversation
> on the plane back from Sarajevo when I'd been
> cartwheeling around the cabin over Peter Riddell's
> piece listing Robin among the very small number

of ministers likely to still be in cabinet in 2005.
And, I'd said, that was because he was quality.
What we'd done was to strip away all the crap, so
that all the public saw was a big player on a big
stage doing serious things.

He was very generous. He said he owed a lot
to me. I gushed about his quality – you can't do
anything without a quality product and that's what
he was. He heaped more praise and gratitude. I
think I have a sharper nose for danger, which is the
right way round. The minister should be pushing
close to the cliff edge, the advisor restraining when
necessary.

We like each other too. I couldn't bear this job if
I didn't like the person I was working for and deep
down want them to succeed.'

This benign mood didn't last. A minister lives with the
consequences of decisions long after they are made. It seemed
impossible for Robin to free himself from the decision taken
reluctantly in his first few weeks to honour an agreement
made by the previous government to supply Hawk jets to the
repressive regime in Indonesia. On 30 August, the people of
East Timor voted for independence from Indonesia. Robin
was very much in favour and so accepted an interview request
from the BBC's most important political programme. The
difficulties that followed are described in a note I made on
12 September:

'The day before I went back to work, Bank Holiday
Monday, Robin did a Today programme interview
on the independence referendum in East Timor.
He felt he had a good story to tell, that Britain had
played a role in persuading Indonesia to put right

24 years of wrong by allowing the people to vote for an end to Indonesian rule. Jim Naughtie asked whether it was true that the Indonesian regime had used Hawk jets to intimidate protestors, despite giving assurances to Britain that they would not be used for repression. Robin had confirmed this in July: two flights, a swift British protest, no more flights. So he said – yes.

It's amazing how stories can take off. I always felt this as a journalist. News isn't what's new, it's what takes off. The story ran quite big that Robin had 'confirmed' that British jets had been used for intimidation, as if his 'confirmation' somehow made him culpable; as if he had himself licensed the jets, whereas they had been licensed by the previous government.

As the Indonesian thugs, ignored by and eventually joined by the army, plunged Timor into bloodshed, the Hawk story ran bigger and bigger. Robin's 'confirmation' locked him into the story as an apparent apologist for the Indonesian regime.

He is the victim of the worst kind of sneering journalism, mostly by broadcasters, but also by some commentators. The premise of their sneering is that our response to tragedy is feeble, but none of them actually advocates British and other soldiers fighting their way up the beaches in the face of 20,000 Indonesian troops. If you're not arguing that, then you've no right to criticise. We can intervene only at the Indonesians' invitation and it is grotesque that journalists should sneer, without acknowledging the hard reality of our position.

Actually, I think the general public is probably much more sensible about it, but I hardly ever talk to a real member of the general public, so I don't know.

Throughout this fortnight, the Hawk story has kept coming back round. Though this government has licensed no jets, it decided in 1997 not to revoke the existing licences. Hawks continue to be delivered, so to that extent you can't blame the critics. Robin lost that argument in '97 – as he loses all arms sales arguments – and has loyally defended it and refrained from briefing against it: as always. He takes the blame and puts up with it.

I suggested suspending supplies until the crisis is over and Robin liked the idea. By yesterday morning, we were under fierce pressure from the Sundays and Robin was trying to get through to Tony Blair to urge suspension. He asked me to try Alastair. Alastair was sympathetic – 'I know it's not a comfortable position you're in'.

We were running out of time and I had no line to take with Sunday papers, who were asking what Robin would be saying at the EU foreign ministers' meeting on Monday, where we expect an embargo on new contracts, but not existing ones. This invited the question – so what are you going to do about the Hawks? Robin had argued at a meeting in the white room at 1CG on Friday afternoon that he would look ridiculous saying he had voted for an arms embargo, but Britain would continue sending Hawks under existing contracts.

When we spoke at 2pm or so on Saturday, he accepted that we were in a hole. He said that if he couldn't talk Blair round, he didn't know what he was going to do at the GAC [General Affairs Committee – jargon for EU foreign ministers].

'The French may block an embargo on existing contracts, in which case I will just keep my head down and let them do it. But if they don't I'll have to block it. I'm not sure I can do that. I think it might have to be a resignation issue.'

I said: 'I was afraid you were going to say that.'

'Why afraid?'

'Because I'm a very selfish person and I like working for you.'

He laughed. It's important to make him laugh.'

In other words, the Foreign Secretary was expected to sit quietly while France blocked the very policy which he wanted to happen: namely, a suspension of arms sales to Indonesia. But if France did not block it, then the Prime Minister would expect Robin to go further and exercise Britain's veto himself, and he might resign rather than veto a policy he personally supported. His principles were close to running aground on the realities of government, that no minister however senior can do as he pleases against the Prime Minister's wishes. There is a sound democratic principle underlying this: that the Prime Minister is the person most visibly accountable to the public for all the government's actions, principles, beliefs, compromises, successes and failures, promises kept or broken. But on the other hand, Cabinet ministers are elected too, and unless they believe strongly in some of their policies, they have little democratic value. There has to be a limit to how much a minister is prepared to compromise in order to stand by at least a few things he believes in. Robin Cook believed it to be wrong to supply arms to dictators, and to continue doing so against evidence that British weapons had been used for oppression. It was one thing to compromise on the guidelines that he had issued after difficult discussions with Number Ten in 1997 (before my time); but quite another to vote on Britain's behalf for continued supplies to a regime trying to suppress

a democratic movement. In practice, once a minister gets
into the position Robin was in that weekend in September
1999, he or she has a harsh choice between unheroic retreat
or resignation; unless he can persuade the PM to change his
mind.

> 'Robin rang back. He had persuaded Blair. I rang
> every Sunday paper. I could hardly believe we had
> got it – Pam [my wife] said at one stage, you can't
> help wondering if you've misunderstood. I hadn't.
> Alastair had rung to say – you announce it. And I'd
> read him our statement.
>
> I was naive enough to think that, because we'd
> pulled off such a coup – stopping these wretched
> exports – we'd get credit. But the papers were vile
> about it. They called it a U-turn and the critics
> regarded it as a meaningless gesture, too late.
>
> I can see their point. Of course it was wrong
> to let the exports go on in 1997. But it was not
> Robin's policy. He was hobbled, from the start of
> his ministerial career, by a decision that was bound
> in the end to haunt him.
>
> Our position feels all wrong. He is defending an
> indefensible policy. I don't blame him. It's absurd
> to argue, as some do, that you should resign rather
> than defend policies you disagree with. Robin has
> done things worth doing. But for him, we would
> tonight still be exporting Hawks. But, looked at
> from the outside, our position is horrible.'

I now read what I wrote then without pride. I don't think
I meant, in the heat of that difficult time, that it is always
absurd to expect a minister to resign rather than take
responsibility for things he opposes. Of course there has to

be a line, and that line cannot be drawn according to pre-set criteria, but by how it feels when you come to it. Looking back on this episode, in the context of Robin's whole career, I think it shows that by making compromises, he was able to achieve some things he believed in, which would not have happened had he resigned. In this case, he got the outcome he believed in, suspension of arms supplies to an unpleasant dictatorship. That would not have happened without Robin Cook being Foreign Secretary.

The battle left him in low spirits.

'He rang this morning and said he wished he'd taken the NATO job. He said the worst of it was that they were again treating him as someone who might get the sack and was totally dependent on Blair's goodwill, whereas in the summer he was treated as a big player who stood for something.

I said I knew it wasn't my role to be glum, but I couldn't help it.

He said: "If you can think of anything to cheer me up, ring."

I said: "Don't expect a call."

He rang this afternoon while I was out for a walk. He asked me to brief the *Guardian* on his role: make clear he had always wanted to stop the Hawks. It was very uncomfortable. Ian Black [Middle East Editor] didn't take it well. He thinks Robin has not delivered the liberal position. He's right, although no conceivable alternative Foreign Secretary would have even fought for it. And, as of tonight, we're no longer exporting Hawks to Indonesia. The job's worth doing: just.'

We then learned that a delivery of Hawks happened to be on the way already, though the media didn't yet know this.

> 'When we first realised there was a delivery of three Hawk jets on the tarmac in the Far East, in transit to Indonesia, I rang Robin and begged him to intervene. He was on his way out of Tokyo to the airport [doing a Far East tour, with the Head of News, Kim Darroch, accompanying]. I thought the spectacle of Hawks arriving in the midst of carnage would be terminal.
>
> That warning looked increasingly prophetic during last week, as Kim remarked at one highly dangerous point.
>
> In Tokyo Robin had decided that (a) we were legally powerless to intervene and (b) would get no credit if we leant on British Aerospace; only odium if we tried and failed. I didn't agree, but didn't push it. He may have been right. I don't know. We soon heard that one of the pilots was diplomatically ill and that Number Ten had been in touch with BAe. I discussed the issue, elliptically and carefully, a couple of times with BAe's press operation, saying that "we're both in the same business, dealing with the same problem."
>
> So the problem hung over us. The media were bound to find out.
>
> While we were waiting for this disaster, the situation on the ground improved, with Habibie and Wiranto [Indonesian leaders] agreeing to a UN peacekeeping force. The media refused to focus on anything but Hawks.
>
> *The Times* produced a dreadfully misleading story that made it look as though the DTI had loaned Indonesia millions to help pay for the Hawks. The

intro was angled on Robin, not Steve Byers or Peter Mandelson, who had been at the DTI at the time. The BBC went into meltdown. John Sergeant, normally so cool, rang to say hysterically: "Your ethical foreign policy is in ruins."

Actually, he wasn't wrong. But it wasn't in ruins because of reality; it was in ruins because of the media perception of reality. They have reached a point at which ethical foreign policy is referred to as a kind of state of perfection.

Robin was understandably cast down. This all happened on Wednesday. I was due to leave for my truncated recce of the State Visit to Africa, in a taxi at 4.30pm. Robin had been at a Cabinet awayday at Chequers. When he got back, at 4.10pm, he called me up to his room and asked me not to go. "I need you here."

While flattering, this was exasperating, not least for all the people who've put in the work to set the recce up.

Next morning, Robin said: "I can't see a way out of this."

I said I wasn't prepared to abandon hope. I used that as a text for a piece/interview/speech that I felt he ought to make, defending his stance. He didn't like the idea. He let his special advisors persuade him it was too defensive. It was defensive, but I think he's got to make the case. He can't keep leaving it unanswered.

On Friday evening he rang from his car, somewhere in Scotland, for a long conversation punctuated by silences, as he wrangled with himself, using me as just someone to listen to his agonised thought process.

He said: "It would be grotesque if I were swept

out of office on this issue, when we've actually got
a good story to tell."

I said I didn't accept the premise. But my words
down the line to Japan the week before last keeping
echoing.'

Robin survived. There were no facts in this news story –
no mistakes made – on which to bring him down, only the
re-surfacing of the damaging impression that his principles
and his policies were way out of line, thanks to the hubristic
phrase 'ethical dimension', long unspoken, but still attached
to the Foreign Secretary. I wrote in my end of 1999 reflection:

'You have to work inside the weirdly-distorted hall-
of-mirrors world of media/politics to understand
how the savagery of machete-wielding militias on
the other side of the world can be blamed on the
British Foreign Secretary.

The Mail's sudden discovery of the freedom
movement in East Timor would have been funny,
but for the genuine suffering on the ground and the
political pain for Robin.

What Robin actually did was to fly to New
Zealand to play his usual deal-brokering role
at a summit which agreed to send Australian
peacekeepers in.

Instead of getting credit, Robin was treated as if
the continued delivery of Hawks, and the MoD's
crass invitation to the Indonesians to a Surrey
arms fair at the height of the barbarity, made him
personally responsible for the orgy of murder.

He found this hard to take calmly, and so did I.
In fact, this episode got me down more than any

in my 18 months. The criticism was wearyingly wrongheaded. And, of course, we were defending decisions Robin had fought against (continued delivery of Hawks) or not been consulted on (the arms fair).'

Every tussle with Number Ten runs down a minister's reserves of goodwill. The more often a minister fights for a policy he values, every time he argues about issues of little interest to the PM, support drains a little more. Number Ten looks for quiet competence. Quiet was something we couldn't achieve – foreign policy has a habit of happening all around you, setting problems that can't be wished away.

Out of nowhere came controversy over a state visit by the Chinese President in October 1999. The accusation was that the Metropolitan Police had helped keep human rights protestors out of the President's sight, at the request of the Chinese embassy. This was another episode in which principles – support for human rights – seemed to come a poor second to policy: welcoming the Chinese leader as a symbol of strengthening friendship with the future superpower. And it was another case where the facts were hard to establish. There were television pictures of a policeman apparently discussing the placing of crowd barriers with a Chinese official. I asked for all relevant officials to be called together to find out what had happened. The head of the security operation explained that there has to be co-ordination between Metropolitan Police and the embassy of a visiting leader, but it is only co-ordination, not, as alleged, the Met taking instructions. By now though the 'fact' was well established that the Foreign Office had colluded with the Met and the Chinese in making sure protestors were confined to places where they could not get near the President. The Foreign

Secretary was under media fire. This note is from 23 October 1999:

> 'We've had a dreadful week, through no fault of our own. The State Visit by the Chinese president was dogged by demonstrations. The policing was heavy-handed. From the right, the *Daily Mail* affected to be as outraged as the left. We were caught in the middle. Poor old Ethical Foreign Policy took another beating.
>
> How do we get ourselves into these messes? Are there not enough unforeseeable, uncontrollable dilemmas in the world, without us creating some of our own?
>
> Events conspired, as usual. On Monday, we had a very successful Commonwealth meeting which expelled Pakistan in response to the military coup [which brought General Musharaf to power]. The media contrived to attack us for not taking account of the unsavoury nature of the deposed – but democratic – government. Imagine the howls if Robin had said: "This is a good military coup, run by enlightened generals – never mind the ballot box." This was, roughly, the line of attack in TV and radio interviews.
>
> On the World Tonight, Robin was repeatedly asked why we were being tough on Pakistan but not on China – the visit was starting the next day. We still don't have a consistent, coherent message to cover the many complexities of a human rights policy in the real world of trade and power. I am working on it.
>
> We went off air on the Tuesday, despite pressure

from Number Ten to get out there and justify the State Visit. We sheltered behind convention, but in truth we were keeping heads down.

Alastair wasn't having it. He pitched into me – good-naturedly, but aggressively – at his Wednesday morning meeting (now moved to an elegant little study in Number Ten, instead of the cavernous echo chamber in the Cabinet Office).

'What's all this bollocks about convention?'

I explained that it wasn't just convention, although we have in the past been hammered for dickering with Royal convention. It was a matter of tactics.

'This is the coverage we were always going to get. The media aren't interested in State Visits, except to destroy them. They don't care about trade, or China. There are demonstrators on the streets and that's the story.'

He wouldn't accept that there was little to be gained and much to be lost by fielding a minister. I promised to put it to Robin.

He was not keen, but neither was he adamant. I left a message with Alastair. Robin's main argument was that if a minister breathed a word of criticism, the Chinese would take offence, and 'we would move from embarrassment, to disaster'. Nevertheless he lost the argument. John Battle was set up for a run of eight lunchtime interviews.

I went down to Millbank to prepare him. I said: "Try not to use any adjectives. Say nothing quotable. Be bland. Just say enough to have your face on the bulletins. Don't criticise the police, but don't get dragged too far into defending them.

That's about as hard a brief as you can have."

He did it. It was a good performance.

Robin said at one point to Alastair, and again to me yesterday: "Why do we have these State Visits? They either attract no coverage, or do damage."

Quite. Once again, we stand vividly accused of failing to measure up to our principled rhetoric. This is becoming too consistent and there will be more to come, probably on the State Visit to Africa.'

There are some who disapprove of press officers giving the sort of advice to elected ministers which I gave to John Battle that day. This in my view would be fine if we lived in a parallel media universe. 'Do you have any comment to make on the policing of the state visit, Minister? Thank you.' It wouldn't be healthy if we had that kind of media. But if democracy involves the grilling of ministers on television, then they have a right to be well prepared for it. Here was a minister, John Battle, of thorough decency, with a serious grip of his policy brief (Robin had been wrong to oppose his appointment), who was required at almost no notice to go and face an interview that might have been set in a Broadcasting Technique class as an impossible exercise. Still new to foreign policy, and never having been in the front line of major controversy, having had no responsibility for the State Visit's policing, he was expected to avoid upsetting China, or offending Buckingham Palace, or criticising the police, or defending the police in terms that seemed to excuse restrictions on peaceful demonstrators. Had he erred one inch into any of those potential errors, he would have brought a storm of media criticism down on the government. It was very much to John Battle's credit that he willingly took on this task and conducted himself with dignity, happy to take advice on where the wolves were lurking and how not to attract their attention.

When the media is on the hunt, there needs to be someone in the team who knows how to protect innocent people from getting hurt. In finding out what had really happened between the police and the Chinese embassy, I judged the pivotal security official to be a patently honest public servant doing a difficult job diligently, with no idea why his actions were suddenly controversial. I felt strongly that he and his colleagues did not deserve to be exposed to unwarranted criticism, but should be defended professionally against media attack.

I felt the same about a leading official on China policy who cried after a harrowing session with Robin Cook, who could be very harsh, I have to say. I found during this episode, and many subsequently, that the only person in a position to find out what had actually happened, judge how valid criticisms were, admit fault if necessary, and defend people from unjust attack, was the press secretary.

I loved the job, including the pressure – in some ways, I loved the pressure most of all, relished facing up to it, however demanding – but around this time found it hard to sustain. Here is a note dated 23.10.99, during another crisis, this time over France refusing to lift a ban on British beef at the end of the period in which our meat exports had been barred because of a cattle disease. France's refusal to re-admit British imports escalated into a major trade row, with some British supermarkets taking French produce off their shelves.

> 'Sunday morning. I am worried about myself, worried enough to have taken a long weekend, which hasn't quite worked: there was a Saturday

afternoon/evening crisis – not a bad one, but critical enough to end the relaxation achieved over the previous 24 hours.

I've been feeling pretty bad: tired, tense, self-pitying, waking up at 4.24am and thinking about it, resenting it. Since returning from the summer holidays I have in two months had only one straightforward 'coasting' day. Otherwise it's been relentless, either dealing with a hard problem, or meeting after meeting of preparation for preventing problems. I'm doing many more meetings, somehow, and finding paper harder to read because it has to be skimmed so fast in the small gaps in the day. That leads to a constant sensation of skimming in haste over potential mistakes, which will take days, weeks, or months to rectify. Actually, we can't afford a real mistake. Robin's doing well, but we used up all our lives, I think.'

Here's an example of my day:

7.45 Hurried reading of cuttings and a few essential papers, while listening to Today programme and preparing lines to take on the beef crisis (very threatening issue, maximum danger approaching)
9.00 At Alastair's meeting, I offer Robin's services as Cabinet spokesman on beef, going through lines I have written and adding AC's good suggestions.
9.30 Dictate lines to Pat and take up to Robin so he can take them to Cabinet.
10.00 Press office daily meeting, explaining beef crisis dangers and listening alertly for other hidden dangers as press officers go through issues of the day.

10.30 Write 'hard questions' Q&A for Robin's round of lunchtime media (this is all my idea, incidentally, no-one else thought he ought to have his head above the parapet, but I thought he would look cowardly not doing so. He agreed)

11.00 Work with Pat on preparations for State Visit to Africa, something we have delayed and delayed until further delay is dangerous.

11.30 Robin returns from Cabinet. Brief him on three key points to make and hard questions to watch for.

12.00-1.00 Tour of Millbank studios. Constant fear of one false word, but he does it superbly.

1.00 Watch and listen to result on the bulletins. It comes out well. Surprised to find how worried I was.

1.30 Walk across park for sandwich, eat at desk while reading papers and trying to catch up. Phone calls, etc.

2.15 Dictate Robin's beef quotes to Pat, for press office to put out.

2.30 Meeting to finalise very difficult written answers on China (dangerous issue)

3.15 Cup of tea, essential papers, phone calls.

3.30 General chat, across the board, with Peter Hain. Highly enjoyable and stimulating, but demanding.

4.15 Summoned from Hain's office to go to Robin's and take him through the difficult China questions. First chance to get to grips with him on this – long overdue. He has to be familiar with the dangers.

4.50 Catch up with Pat on what I've missed and must do.

5.00 Meeting chaired by John Kerr on 'China –

lessons learned'. Called at my instigation to make hard points that I know they don't want to hear about how we have to improve our performance on big, potentially damaging public events.

6.30 Catch up with Pat, agree what I must do tonight and what I will do down the phone from home tomorrow. Huge box of paper to read. Skim fast and leave what I can for another day.

7.00 To private office to break various pieces of bad news they need to know about.

7.20 Leave office a shade late for train.

7.50 Miss train, catch slow one. Read papers to prepare for what I must do down the phone in the morning, before starting long weekend.

8.45. Home. Nice dinner with Pam.

Conclusion: a badly crowded day, a bit worse than usual, but not that unusual. At least we stayed upright.

I spent all Friday morning working, though not hard (note to Peter Hain on proposed 'core message'; more State Visit planning) and then had a marvellous three hour walk in the mellow autumn light.

Yesterday I had a lovely morning shopping for wine and food and books, had an hour's walk in mellow ditto and then found myself plunged into a China-related problem that would be too tedious to relate, but which involved two calls to Robin and some difficult, delicate decisions about how to defuse things before a mild irritation became something to regret.'

Looking back from the safe distance of more than a decade later, I like my reference to the 'hall-of-mirrors world of media/politics.' It has more meanings than I can have intended in a quick note at the time. The intended meaning was that from inside government, the media reflects back at you some alarmingly distorted images. One of the tasks of the spokesperson/media advisor is to anticipate how a minister's straightforward, upright actions will look when the public sees them in the distorted mirror. This was not a pun on my last destination in journalism, the *Daily Mirror*, but on the whole media. It was telling that in this feverish episode, the most heated phone call I received was from one of the most staid figures in political journalism, which John Sergeant was at the time. As Alastair Campbell had said in Sarajevo, even the old-fashioned figures of serious broadcasting were being dragged along by the more hysterical elements of the media. It was a peculiar thing that as television became increasingly the dominant way people received their news, the more the broadcasters allowed themselves to defer to the newspapers' agenda.

This was more than a puzzling irritant, it had serious implications on issues of national importance like Europe, and still does in the age of instant communication through the internet. The least modern part of the media – newspapers – have retained their grip on defining what news is, day by day.

Another meaning of hall-of-mirrors was the element of fairground mayhem in which the British Foreign Secretary was trying to do a serious job. Other fairground metaphors apply. There were times when government seemed to have as little control as a dodgem car buffeted by bank holiday hooligans.

Alastair Campbell may have been at the far end of frustration as he cursed the lobby, but he was not entirely wrong about the atmosphere in which the media and government were conducting their aggressive transaction at the time. The newspapers were not entirely to blame. Alastair, and Tony Blair himself, with Peter Mandelson and Gordon Brown playing their parts, had been too successful and at times too cynical in their often brilliant manoeuvres in the media. Journalists were long fed up with it, and didn't mind taking revenge, or simply rebelling against the line they were given. Robin Cook was to some extent a victim of this media mood as the novelty of the Blair government soured. It wasn't that the media had anything in particular against him – most correspondents liked and admired him, and had a touch of sympathy as they buffeted his dodgem car – but he was a big figure in a domineering government and was unfortunate enough to show vulnerability.

There was no point complaining about it and I don't think I did, to the media. Calling it a hall of mirrors was to an extent my way of not taking it absolutely seriously. Seeing the absurdity of it was a way of coping. It was also a professional necessity. You had to be able to anticipate and deal with the distortions and the farce, as part of the trade of government. To regard it all as too absurd to be worth bothering about was a temptation which some civil servants fell for, though not all; a small minority I would say, though at times they happened to be in key positions. To give Sir John Kerr his due, he understood and acted on the obligation to take seriously media opinion as a rough reflection of public opinion. There were many senior diplomats in my time at the FCO who saw that however ridiculous the media's attitudes might seem, they are the channel through which most people see and hear what is being done in their name by government. So the news has to be taken seriously, not because government has been corrupted by spin, but because government which sees the media as beneath contempt is not fulfilling the duty to explain. This is a fundamental democratic duty, and it is inadmissible to regard the media as impossibly trivial: if that's how they are, if that's what people want to buy and read, that's their right. Being accountable to the public through the media and parliament is profoundly important in a democracy, and can't be ignored because newspapers and backbenchers often see trivialities as the main event. It is not a good reflection on our country that accountability goes through distorting mirrors, but that doesn't make the sometimes undignified process unimportant.

It is difficult to hang on to this democratic thread, the importance of government publicly accounting for itself, during crazed episodes inflicted by the media. It is dangerous to become so pressured that you start to hold the media in contempt. I was shocked by Alastair Campbell's black mood on that day in Sarajevo, because I had always found him cheerfully robust, quite amazingly so at times. I think I was always aware that I had no right to hate the media, as I must have seemed like a hooligan on the dodgems when John Major's government was being pilloried by the political media (in my *Standard* days, never mind the *Mirror*).

Perhaps there was never a golden age in the relationship between politics and the media, though as a young journalist I used to enjoy listening to my mentor, Robert Carvel of the Evening Standard, describing tea and toast with Attlee, or watching Winston Churchill's decline. Churchill was very ill during his second period at Number Ten, but the extent of the ageing Prime Minister's illness was not explained, in a more deferential age. Is it a fair trade – less deference, a coarser, even thuggish media, for greater openness, more public knowledge, greater pressure on those in power? I think so, though our democracy would be healthier if some newspapers thought a little more deeply about their role as guardians of what the public gets to know. I won't claim to have thought profoundly about this during a career in journalism that included chairmanship of the political journalists at Westminster. But I do think about it, and worry about it, with the hindsight wisdom of having been on both sides of this rough trade.

The coarsening of political journalism has been part of the cheapening of the media: not just the obsession with glamour in the tabloids, but the glibness of the 'two-way' in broadcasting: that is, a presenter interviewing a reporter in an atmosphere of breathless brevity that releases either from any obligation to go beyond cliche.

Working closely for the Foreign Secretary, I had stepped through the distorting mirror, from one side to the other, trying to keep a useful sense of perspective about both my professions, government and journalism.

Being on the other side of the mirror was at times unreal, never more so than when in the Royal party.

Six
Does The Queen Use A Mouse?

October 1999 brought a State Visit to Ghana, followed by the Commonwealth Heads of Government meeting in South Africa. This is what I wrote at the time:

'I was first to arrive at the Royal Suite. The ladies in waiting turned up in an atmosphere of semi-holiday. The Queen's private secretary [Robin Janvrin]: a handsome 50ish man with the soft voice and considerate air of a discreet GP. A conversational manner of smiling hesitancy, which concealed a sharp, shrewd mind. Professionally pleasant and probably genuinely pleasant too. On the plane, the uniforms hanging in economy class, the hatboxes stowed at the back of the business lounge, the deputy sergeant footman squatting on the floor polishing shoes. A cheery, pugnacious Welsh redhead who looked and sounded more like a scrum half than a valet. He returned my shoes shining like they hadn't shone since leaving the shop window, and my suits with a crease you could cut yourself on.

Coming out of the plane into the glow of a hot African sunset, standing at the top of the steps, with The Queen and The Prince already at the foot of the steps. Stopping on the tarmac for the national anthems. Into buses with private secretaries and ladies in waiting and high commission staff. The convoy breaking up in the huge crowds. The fretful ride to the reception, behind schedule, jammed in traffic. The receiving line. Shaking hands with the president whose K you have vetoed (my small gesture to human rights).'

One of the diplomatic curiosities into which I was initiated was the awarding of honours to mark Royal visits. It was traditional for the host to be honoured, in this case a knighthood for President Rawlings of Ghana. When he first came to power in 1979, he had eight generals executed. I pointed out the controversy that would follow if he were knighted. He was not.

'At the reception, the detectives passing messages about Miss Ghana 1999 down the little mikes in their cuffs. Waking early and walking along the shining sands beside the Labadi Beach Hotel. At the Durbar, sitting in the shade and telling the Foreign Sec and the Queen's private sec that we're OK for the moment, though I know Nick Witchell [BBC Royal correspondent] thought the democracy passage in the Queen's speech to parliament strong, so I'll get news dept to monitor the bulletins with care. Ringing home is difficult – every time I start a conversation down the mobile there is a burst of drumming or native song.'

Nick Witchell was right: President Rawlings was offended by the applause given by parliament when the Queen commended

Ghana's transition to democracy. Actually, this passage was a deserved tribute to Rawlings for handing over power to a genuinely elected successor: the election was imminent. The problem was that the applause sounded to him like applause for his departure. This illustrates the extreme delicacy of the Queen's speeches abroad. Robin Cook, Robin Janvrin, I and FCO Africa people had worked carefully on this speech, but failed to spot that it might be taken as anything but praise for transition to democracy. Rawlings made his feelings known through his Foreign Minister during the noisy Durbar after the speech. Robin came down from the official stand and said to me: 'We have a problem.'

My note:

> 'In private office, Robin explained to Sherard, me and Sir Robin Janvrin that Rawlings felt our high commissioner was hostile and wanted him withdrawn. Whatever the rights and wrongs, we were in a fix. We couldn't afford to have Rawlings make his feelings public. We decided to craft a tribute to him in the Queen's toast to the State Banquet that Robin could show to the Foreign Minister, who would calm Rawlings. But it would have to be not too fulsome, or the British media would be on our backs. On the way to the banquet, in the bus, Janvrin showed me the finished product: the Queen had changed only one word of our combined labour.
>
> Then there was the problem of honours. I had intervened weeks before to argue against giving Rawlings the knighthood he wanted. I had won. Now the question was whether to make the usual award of a knighthood to the British High Commissioner

at the end of the tour. Janvrin and Sherard both said it had become too routine. They agreed – Sir Robin Janvrin, KCVO, and Sherard Cowper-Coles, CMG LVO – that gongs were sprayed about too liberally. Robin kept giving me ironic looks.

Arriving at the Sheraton, Pretoria, straight to private office and down to work. Someone says: 'It's amazing the way you guys just walk in and start working, as if working never stops.' It doesn't.

We're sitting talking to Robin and Gaynor, when Janvrin comes in with a clean version of The Queen's speeches (South African State Banquet; Chogm – Commonwealth heads of government meeting – opening ceremony) which he, Robin, Sherard and I have re-worked on the plane. They are now very good, though we say it ourselves.

I wake early, take a book out on to the balcony, and watch the distant hills take shape in the dawn and then take on the colour of Africa, a parched brown. I read the cuttings.

Lining up for the presentation to President Mbeki, the Equerry joins the line at the end. I usually go at the end. I say: 'Don't confuse the Queen. She knows the last one is the spokesman. Second to last is the Foreign Secretary's private secretary.'

The Queen gets it right. But the Duke, introducing Mrs Mbeki, gets confused.

'This is the Foreign Secretary's private secretary and...the private secretary's private secretary.'

He makes it sound like a joke. Perhaps it is.

Sherard: 'No, Sir, he's my ADC.'

When the guns go off for the 21-gun salute, they are so close, we are all shocked. The media say the

Queen was the first to recover her composure.

At a school in Alexandra, uniformed children sing beautifully. I ring Pam and say: 'Just listen.'

The tour was crucial for Robin because this was the kind of high-profile event that could easily have gone wrong, and created more question-marks over his judgement or future, had we let it: and particularly if the media had sensed a schism between Robin and the Queen. This was the high-stakes background to the day-to-day routine of the press office:

> 'Janvrin says: 'John, I wonder if you wouldn't mind re-reading The Queen's Chogm speech against the Foreign Secretary's Commonwealth Society speech to make sure there aren't common phrases the media can spot.'
>
> Janvrin is shrewd, a top class pro.
>
> On the plane I mark up the speeches, finding four alarmingly similar passages. It's hard to do this while eating lunch. I get caviar on the Queen's speech.
>
> I'm worried about a line in it which talks about using a mouse [personal computers were a novelty then]. Janvrin's line is too good to drop – we know it will make the bulletins.
>
> I say: 'Does the Queen ever use a mouse?'
>
> 'No.'
>
> 'The media will ask.'
>
> 'I think we should be robust about that.'
>
> Janvrin prevails. The speech works, the soundbite makes the bulletins. The media doesn't mind.
>
> As we're coming down to land, I'm clearing with Robin a short, sharp statement on the charges

brought by the Pakistan military regime against the arrested premier, so that we can set the pace on a difficult story. I only just make it back to my seat for landing. Earlier in the tour, Sherard had been caught out and landed sitting on a red box.

In the Hilton, private office was a cramped room piled with boxes of fax paper, crammed with too many chairs. Pat [who had flown out to join me for Chogm as I wasn't allowed support on a Royal visit] said I looked worn out. Robin did the Today programme down the line from my bedroom.

I worked through lunch, at a series of bilaterals: Zimbabwe, India, Kenya. Andrew Patrick, the private secretary, and I fell on the sandwiches uneaten by the foreign ministers.

Alastair Campbell wanted me to join him for a briefing. I went up to Number Ten's palatial private office – with balcony – but he was asleep, having written his script. I never had time. Pat said that when we walked on stage, she thought – John's not prepared for this. I got by through a combination of deliberate dullness and knowledge gleaned from the bilaterals. Robin Oakley said: 'It's very funny seeing you and Alastair up there together.'

We again worked well into the evening. Pat rebelled against another meal in the hotel, so we went down to the Tropicana and ate a buffet dinner, followed by beers and pool in a bar round the corner.'

I also recorded a flash of why Robin could evoke such loyalty in those who knew him up close:

'At the Queen's reception, Robin introduced Pat to the Queen as 'the brains behind John Williams.'

Sherard, Pat and I went to the Remembrance Day ceremony at the cenotaph in central Durban. It was punishingly hot. Sherard whispered: 'I think I might faint.'

I whispered to Pat: 'What about you?'

'Me too.'

When we got back to the hotel, Pat and I went for a swim. Then Sherard – in shorts – gathered us all up to go to a game reserve. It was a long, nice bus ride through the kind of country you remember from books and films set in the veldt. We saw rhino, giraffe, buffalo, monkeys. It came on to rain and the earth smelled marvellously of moisture seeping into the dry land. Sherard can be very funny. It felt like a nice team. Pity we do this only rarely. We were eating cucumber sandwiches on a verandah when I looked up and noticed the roof was crawling with tarantulas. I scarpered, to much laughter.

We had all hoped to knock off a quick bit of work, change and go out to eat. But John Kerr came in with the bad news that the human rights stuff that we wanted in the communique wasn't there: Blair hadn't fought hard enough for it. We sat and chewed this over with Robin, to no great effect, for ages.

Pat had meanwhile set up a little party that we'd had an idea for, taking over Number Ten's luxuriously spacious and now vacant private office, with its 14th floor balcony [the PM had left]. We ordered a couple of bottles of champagne as our treat for the team.

We worked hard on the final day, setting up a little press conference and phoning people right down to the last moment. Pat was packing up around me in private office as I was briefing people. We had a last leisurely lunch and then the buses took us to the airport. There I was cornered by Robert Hardman *[Daily Mail* royal correspondent], who had tumbled to the fact that we'd lost some vital bits from the communiqué.'

Many, perhaps most, international meetings end with platitudinous communiqués from which all substance has been strained by the need for everyone to have a text with which they can agree. So they achieve nothing, except to avoid offence. The exception is the European Union, where the circumlocutions of the draft communiqué are coded references to frictions and fissures over the issues of live controversy and have lasting significance for each country's strategic interests. Every few years, the EU plunges itself into decision-making that cannot be fudged by well-crafted text, the battle has to be fought. The Union was heaidng into such a battle in 2000.

Seven
Critical Engagement

Europe was a regular source of friction between the Foreign Secretary, Prime Minister and Chancellor. There was personal friction between Robin Cook and Gordon Brown, as well as a serious difference of opinion over joining the euro. Cook was in favour, Brown against. Though Tony Blair was in favour, he was more cautious than Robin, and had to take account of his Chancellor's opposition, which was a strong theme in a bigger story, the often creative and in the end destructive relationship between Tony Blair and Gordon Brown. All other politicians of the time were minor characters in this drama.

Robin Cook was positioned at a particularly exposed place where the personal and strategic interests of Blair and Brown collided. At this stage the euro was the issue on which the differences between the two were most obvious: it was only later that the government became divided across the range of challenges it faced, between Blair and Brown. A more cautious politician would have decided therefore to stay out of the argument about the euro. But Robin Cook was determined to push the government towards joining the euro, as part of his increasingly strong identity as a champion of Europe. A cannier politician would have decided to avoid taking on those newspapers most hostile to Europe, which happened to be the newspapers which inflicted most pain on politicians in trouble. But Robin Cook was not content to survive – hard though that had been – he wanted to shape the big events of the time. He had spent too long in Opposition to be content with office for the sake of being there: he wanted to achieve something lasting. And on a personal level he was ready to try to re-establish himself as a major figure.

Europe was in the process of uniting the old east and west in a Union from Poland to Portugal, from the Atlantic to beyond the fallen Iron Curtain. He saw this as historic, even noble, with Britain taking a constructive role, settling old arguments about Britain's place in the world as a leading power in the new Europe of democracies. But staking out this high ground involved a lot of bruisingly low politics. I noted on 27 November 1999:

> 'Robin finally gave the Euro speech trailed several weeks ago on the front of *The Times*. David Clark [special advisor]'s draft was too strong for me, never mind to get through the Treasury or Number Ten. Gordon Brown sulked and refused to clear it. Jonathan Powell neutered it. He argues that 'the case is made' – with approval of the EU falling all the time.'

By this, I meant – how does Jonathan think the case is made when approval for the EU is falling? I think his point simply was – we don't need an argument about Europe, thanks. This note is the first mention of an important figure in Robin's story, David Clark. Special advisors are there to give Cabinet ministers advice on the party political aspects of government policy, to liaise with the parliamentary party, to remind ministers of where they come from politically, to put that into the mix of policy discussion, and to speak for the minister on his political approach to government issues. In some cases, the special advisors have difficult relationships with the government spokespeople, but not in mine. David Clark was fully supportive of my efforts to revive and then maintain the Foreign Secretary's fortunes in the media. In fact, when a junior minister, Keith Vaz, got into media trouble and asked how Robin had dealt with Sandline, David told him: 'We sent for John Williams.' I tell that not out of vanity but to show that David and I were very close – personally warm as well as professionally solid. I respected his role as Robin's partisan champion, as much as David respected mine as the cautious operator. I enjoyed working with him while being occasionally exasperated, as he must have been with me at times: we both, I think, recognised that the mix was important. Too cautious, too bland: not for Robin. Too partisan, too politically aggressive, especially against Gordon Brown: end of Robin.

We had slightly but significantly different approaches to Europe. That was good. It must be disastrous for a serious politician to have a team of advisors all saying yes. We disputed, creatively. But David was at times reckless, I felt, just as he must have felt that I was, at times, too tight.

I noted at the end of 1999:

> 'Robin first said way back in January or February that he was thinking of making a move on the Euro and wanted to discuss it. We never did get to discuss it, until an office meeting immediately after the summer holidays. What Robin had decided was to make a pro-Euro statement from Japan.
>
> He asked me to write some phrases and I suggested: 'We won't let Britain lose out by staying out.'
>
> He was making the speech on a Monday. David

Clark and I were to agree a media line and farm it out between us on the Sunday. We waited and waited for Gordon Brown's approval for the speech. It came late and grudgingly. The speech made a real impact.

Apart from sharpening the government's message, it got the lobby interested in Robin again as a big player in Cabinet, as opposed to Foreign Secretary.

Robin had discussed his plans with Blair at Chequers a few days before, but I don't know how much he had told him. That morning I was at Alastair's morning meeting at Number Ten. He was called away to see the Prime Minister. As I left, Alastair emerged to say: 'That was about your speech. Tony says – cool it.'

Gordon Brown was upset. The irony is that Brown was always the most enthusiastic European, while Robin was the senior Eurosceptic. But Robin has always said that once it exists, we've to go in – as long as it works. He is genuinely convinced we will pay a heavy price once the world thinks we're not going in.

We got a splash in *The Times* – and a flattering profile – by flagging Robin's speech for the newly-launched Britain-in-Europe campaign.

After protracted last minute negotiations, Robin rang to say: 'I'm very annoyed – no, alarmed – at the lack of strategy these conversations have revealed.'

At the start of 2000, the Foreign Secretary called a strategy meeting of ministers, officials and advisors at 1 Carlton

Gardens. I made a note on 8th January.

'At the ministerial meeting, the top item was Europe. Before Christmas, Robin came back from the Helsinki summit exasperated by the media and its parallel-universe coverage of Europe.

I started writing a paper for Robin on how to deal with it. Hearing from Sherard that he was seeing Blair the following day, I tried to get in to see him first. It was one of those days when it just didn't happen, so I doorstepped him [the Foreign Secretary] and walked over to Number Ten, talking him through my suggestions. As he waited for Blair, he read them. Basically, the suggestion was a New Year fightback, using sharp phrases to argue for positive engagement and to persuade the media and public that there is no conflict between engagement and the national interest.

When he came back, he called together Kim and me, John Kerr, David Clark and the three private secretaries (Sheinwald was away – Nigel Sheinwald, Europe Director). He and Blair had agreed to fight back.

This week we have got under way, not without difficulty. The starting point was to be Robin's speech in Lisbon, using some of my sharp phrases. Our worry, as ever, is Number Ten's commitment. I had rung Alastair during the holiday and fixed a meeting to agree the strategy. This was fixed for Wednesday, the ministerial meeting having been Tuesday (at which Kerr described the Europe minute as 'brilliant' – I have heard it described as 'Nigel's famous minute', although everyone knows who wrote the 'message' section). After the ministerial meeting, David Clark spoke to Alice Miles of *The Times*, who had rung to ask what was happening on Europe. David told her about the meeting and some of the strategy, which predictably angered Alastair.

Before seeing Alastair, Kim and I were supposed to talk to Robin. He stood us down, saying he was happy to see us after Alastair. I was pretty uneasy at agreeing tactics on something so big without Robin's prior agreement, or at least his explicit carte blanche. So I doorstepped him again, this time at the start of a Balkans meeting. He said he hadn't written the Lisbon speech and had nothing to give me. I presented him with a chunky Europe passage for agreeing with Alastair and briefing to the lobby that afternoon. He went through it, made a couple of changes and sent me on my way.'

Throughout Robin's time as Foreign Secretary, his antagonistic relationship with the Chancellor, Gordon Brown, was a problem in the background. It came to the foreground whenever Robin Cook made an intervention on Europe. There would have been no avoiding Europe even if the Foreign Secretary had wanted to, but for Robin this was a major issue on which he had a distinctive position that he wanted to highlight. He had become the most enthusiastic pro-European of the big figures in the government, with the exception of Peter Mandelson (who was not always in government, having to resign in 1998, being reappointed in 1999, and having to resign again in 2001: but he was always a major figure in the politics of the time – and not a fan of Robin's). Once Robin Cook had recovered from his early difficulties, he saw Europe as the policy area in which to exert himself and to influence the government's direction. He could not have chosen an issue more likely to put him repeatedly in conflict with Gordon Brown. I don't think it was deliberate. Robin was serious about Britain's place in Europe, believing that a role as one of the main decision-makers in the Union increased Britain's power. This was a conclusion from the Kosovo conflict, in which Tony Blair and Robin Cook had been at the centre of a European policy, having more weight in Washington for their leadership of the European military and diplomatic effort. During Kosovo, Britain was 'at the heart of Europe', in the words of the previous Prime Minister John Major, who had been unable to turn the phrase into reality against the opposition of many in his party.

However, Britain was in a very important sense not at the heart of Europe – outside the newly-formed currency union. Blair was in favour of joining the euro, but allowed Gordon Brown to delay a decision. The Foreign Secretary chafed at the delay, with increasingly public impatience. He knew though that pushing at the edge of government policy on the euro was personally dangerous. Whenever he discussed a possible intervention, he was pulled in two directions, boldness or caution. David Clark and I tended to be counterweights in these discussions – him for boldness, me for caution. There was nothing ideological about my wariness, only a tactical sense of where Robin's words would take him and the Foreign Office on a hugely divisive government policy. I was certainly not taking far-sighted views about the euro's later difficulties after the financial crisis of 2008. I was thinking much shorter-term: judging how far it was legitimate to go within the agreed government policy. A minister either speaks the agreed government policy, or goes beyond it with a very clear knowledge of what he is doing, knowing the career risks; or resigns to speak freely from the backbenches. I never wanted the Foreign Secretary to break out of the agreed policy by accident. It may sound absurd that a Foreign Secretary might accidentally breach his own government's foreign policy. But I had found, moving from journalism to government, that politicians were not always quite so aware of the precise impact of their words as the media supposes. There is always an assumption that every word must be calculated for effect, and of course most are. But both the Foreign Secretaries I worked for at length were at times surprisingly naïve for such seasoned operators – I think genuinely – about the likely effect of things they intended to say, or the embarrassing impact of what they had just said. Robin once made a finely calculated speech about the euro, stepping delicately round every trap, but in the question and answer session said he thought British membership inevitable. He was genuinely surprised when he came off stage, saying to his host: 'Oh dear, look at my press officer's face, I fear I may have said something.' Maybe I was naïve about this, but I don't think so, because when at times Robin did decide to push at the boundary, knowing the likely Brown reaction, he chose the words with great care.

It is hard to recall, after the euro crisis, how close the Blair government seemed to be at times to deciding to join, and how sensitive an issue it was. When journalists interpreted single words as significant signals, they and we were not playing word games, but dancing round one of the most important strategic decisions of recent times. The decision was in the end taken by there being no decision, only a continued dance until the possibility faded. We didn't know that at the time. Every discussion about the euro, every speech and interview, every row that blew up was – looking forwards not back – possibly the beginning of the decisive move.

So policy on the euro lurked behind everything the Foreign Secretary, Prime Minister and Chancellor did on the whole range of EU policy. To speak a little more enthusiastically about Europe than the others was taken as a signal of movement. Sometimes the Prime Minister spoke at least as enthusiastically as his Foreign Secretary, but he didn't like Robin getting too far ahead. The PM had his own difficult relationship with the Chancellor, at that time in the early stages of the deterioration which came to be a great rift in the government. So whatever Robin did or said on Europe was to swim out into the most dangerous political waters.

At this stage, in early 2000, the euro was lurking beneath the surface. The visible issue was the moment due soon when several nations from the former Soviet empire would join the European Union, making the Thatcherite warning of a European superstate more plausible. (The former PM had minted this powerful argument in her final phase, a decade earlier). Our discussions – arguments – were about how to position the government ahead of this moment.

> 'Alastair said he didn't believe we could get a Europe story going now, without it turning into Cook v Brown. I said we could and we did. The coverage was good. Robin has made a New Year mark as Foreign Secretary coming out fighting the

cause for Europe.

Alastair rang that evening to see how I'd got on with the lobby [that is, briefing the Westminister 'lobby' of political correspondents]. Blair is obviously following this closely. John Sawers [private secretary at No 10 for foreign policy] rang the following morning to say Blair had been on the phone from holiday in Portugal to say he didn't want us briefing that he and Robin had agreed on a Cabinet discussion on Europe. I told Sawers I had agreed with Alastair not to do that without agreement.

Yesterday when I spoke to Alastair again, he agreed that the operation had gone pretty well. He and Blair felt we shouldn't brief the Cabinet discussion in advance because it would get too hyped. But Alastair would brief it afterwards. So, at least they are still on board for this operation.

Meanwhile AC likes my plans for drawing in the pro-Europe media for a fight against the Eurosceptic press.

What all this doesn't get across is the sheer volume of stuff I have to deal with, hour by hour. It's been a ludicrously busy week. At times I have two people waiting to talk to me, plus phone calls, and Pat waiting to get on with what I really want to get on with. On Thursday, I began dictating a piece of paper to her at ten and finished it after five, so constant were the interruptions on Pakistan, Iran, Russia and a host of other topics big and small, all potentially dangerous. I love it, of course. Boredom is the great enemy and there's no time for that.'

David Clark was passionate about Europe and partisan in Robin's favour, as he was entitled to be. He found the Prime Minister's caution frustrating, and the Chancellor's attitude both to Robin and to Europe infuriating. We worked well together, but I was becoming concerned that David's briefings to the media were doing the Foreign Secretary harm. Robin did not believe in briefing against others, though he was copiously briefed against.

Once, after a particularly aggravating piece, Robin said: 'Why are we the only boy scouts in Whitehall?'

I said: 'Because you want it that way, don't you?'

'Yes.'

David found it hard to stand back and see Robin run down unattributably, especially by Charlie Whelan, the Chancellor's crude special advisor/spokesman. This was a matter of loyalty and affection as well as of politics. David had a very strong friendship with Robin of a different kind to mine. They had been together a long time, whereas I had come in to do a professional repair job, out of which came a warm relationship. But fond as I was of Robin, I was there to stop mistakes and raise objections that others didn't. It was a role that the former Prime Minister Jim Callaghan had commended as 'the yes-but man', which was in his view essential in government. David respected that and supported it, in fact was always generous in praising the work I was doing, and never in any doubt about the need for it.

Robin Cook was now sufficiently recovered to be able to think not only about shifting the government's position on Europe, but about laying down some broad doctrine on foreign policy. It was time for a major speech giving a broad strategic theme, of a kind foresworn while the only strategy was survival. David Clark and I had done a lot of thinking and talking about this, with Robin's other special advisors, Andrew Hood and David Mathieson. The special advisors had an attractive room with deep sofas and long windows overlooking St James's Park, in which I always spent many hours, chewing things over. And I liked to hang around private office, chatting to the private secretaries and senior officials who came and went. Decisions are not all made on paper and difficulties do not always arise as agenda items at meetings.

This added to the pressure of time when back in my little room, being force fed paper by Pat and presented with phone calls to return and people to find time for. It was only thanks to her fine sense of priorities that I kept on top of what mattered, which wasn't always obvious: between us we had good instincts for what mattered, and enjoyed being too sharp to be caught out.

It was not a game. I did not make myself universally popular as the yes-but man. I took a hostile grilling from officials in Middle East Directorate for pointing out that if Robin went to Tehran – the first Foreign Secretary to do so for 20 years – the visit would be ruined by Iran's decision to persecute a group of Jewish citizens on trumped up charges. Robin must be asked about it and would have to criticise and then the whole tour would be seen as a falling-out, not as a triumph of creative diplomacy. Robin postponed the visit, and in fact never got there (Jack Straw was to do so). I did not for a moment regret being awkward. The officials who resented my intervention would not have to answer for hypocrisy to parliament or the media if Robin went to Iran and failed to speak out. I was beginning to work out that policy is a fascinating game if you don't have to answer for it. The Foreign Secretary does have to. A lot of officials grasped that, but not all, and understanding of the perverse disciplines of democratic government did not always correspond to seniority. The Commons and the newspapers may often seem crude in their arbitrary indignation – I got fed up with them too – but they keep ministers fretfully accountable.

Some senior officials were very much against Robin making a big speech, fearing something as self-defeating as the 'ethical dimension'. But others were keen to see the Foreign Secretary set out some broad themes, for example Tony Brenton, later Ambassador to Russia. Another reason for having avoided major speeches was Robin's writing method. The Foreign Secretary has a speech writer, who is usually a bright young official on the way to a great career. When I started working at the FCO, the speech writer was Matthew Gould, later Ambassador to Israel, a brilliant and engaging young man, then in his 20s, who worked in the room next to me and was full of good ideas well beyond his brief. There are regular speeches – and statements to the Commons – which the speech writer routinely turns out in draft, using briefs from FCO departments, for the Foreign Secretary to add some personal gloss. It is a peculiarly difficult job, having to guess what The Boss (as the office calls him) wants to say, and to find a way of writing in a style that is plausibly his. Robin found it hard to work this way, often insisting on discarding the draft and starting all over again, shutting himself up in his room, pacing around for hours, dictating to the speech writer. This proved so disruptive to his schedule of meetings and to the clearing of paper that Sherard Cowper-Coles, the Principal Private Secretary, developed a deep aversion to the idea of any speech that didn't have to be made. Sherard and I got on well – as on our safari in South Africa – but there was always tension between us about the Foreign Secretary's time. That tends to be the case between private secretary and press secretary. The diary quickly fills, but the press secretary needs time at short notice for quick response and for pause-and-reflect.

At the start of 2000, I thought it was time to find a way of explaining the approach that underlay his different responses to different situations. He had been criticised for Britain not intervening against Russia in Chechnya, but against Serbia in Kosovo, for example. I wrote a note about the process of producing this speech on 29 January 2000.

'The task was not simply to find the right words to explain coherently our differing responses to the real world, but to find a way of getting them into circulation. I suggested a set-piece speech. Robin said: 'I want to make a speech in the New Year about foreign policy priorities and principles. We can put the core message into that.' He decided to do it at Chatham House and did so yesterday.

Kim was dead against, understandably worried that it would be seen as and panned as a speech defending EFP [ethical foreign policy]. I was more optimistic about what we could achieve. [Kim Darroch was still Head of News, with me the deputy.]

My main idea was a phrase about 'doing what we can, wherever we can, however we can' to get across the point that promoting human rights in a complicated world did not mean that you had to make the same response everywhere, that you had to do what might make a difference, that you had to be realistic as well as principled. Robin had to be seen to be defining a workable doctrine for the pursuit of values in a hard world.

My other idea was to say that he rejects the dismal argument that because we can't do everything, we should do nothing.

As a novice bureaucrat, I wasn't sure how this project would proceed. A couple of days before Christmas, Hamish Cowell [who had succeeded Matthew as the speech writer] came in and said Sherard had asked for a speech outline. Had I any thoughts? I asked him to give me half an hour. We needed something to give us some cover, so that it wasn't just a re-working of EFP. I thought of 'pursuing the national interest in the new century'. National interest can mean what you want it to, but it could be made a broad cover for pursuing a system of values.

Robin liked the outline. Then there was a title, which Chatham House needed to put on the invitations. Everyone struggled. In the end Robin and I, talking in the flat at 1CG, came up with 'Foreign Policy and National Interest'.

Two weeks ago, he convened an office meeting to discuss ideas: Kim and I, the two Davids [David Clark and David Matthieson], Sherard, Richard Clarke (head of planners, the office that does the free thinking), Charles Crawford (Balkans expert and general intellectual), Nigel Sheinwald (Europe, ex head of news, and generally sensible person), Robert Cooper (Blair's foreign policy advisor). We all kicked it around for half an hour and were then told to 'go away and write modules that will stimulate my thinking'.

I did a Europe section, attacking the sceptics for pretending to defend the national interest. I hadn't been asked for this. I was supposed to be contributing the core message and some other stuff for Richard's section on 'policy prescription'. Nigel had suggested that we come up with some sort of 'doctrine'. I had a phrase in my head: critical engagement. It seemed to me to cover the good creative things Robin has done (Iran, Libya), as well as the hard things that need defending and explaining (Indonesia, Russia). Pat e-mailed it to Hamish, who wanted to work on the speech overnight last Wednesday/Thursday. He didn't include it in the draft circulated among the speech team. I said I would be grateful if he could add it to the stuff being sent to Robin, who wanted to work on the speech over last weekend at Chevening. I didn't know if Robin had got it, but when the draft came back from Brussels, critical engagement was there. Everyone liked it when we went through the draft next day.

I was by now pessimistic. The *Guardian* had leaked a decision by Blair to overrule Robin and allow Zimbabwe to buy spares for their Hawk aircraft, which have been flying in combat over the Congo, where a nasty war is going on. It was impossible to square this with EFP, or indeed with any decent or sensible policy. It seemed to me that Robin's speech was now bound to be judged as a defence of EFP and he would be found guilty of not delivering.

I had said to Robin that he must decide whether to use the word 'ethical' or not; either way, it was a story. He didn't use it.

The way it has come out is that generally he is

judged to have eased away from EFP, introducing 'critical engagement' as a more realistic term for pursuing national interests and human rights in a pragmatic way. We won't be able to judge for a while. But for the moment it feels like a good piece of re-positioning. He has already re-positioned himself as the Cabinet's leading European. Taken together with the verdict that he's come through his difficulties, there's a chance that we can use 2000 to re-establish him as a big figure. But that means no mistakes, a lot of work and a good deal of finesse.'

Eight
A Stronger Robin In A Wider Europe

Along with 'critical engagement', the Foreign Secretary developed a theme of Britain as the 'champion of enlargement'. Enlargement was the clumsy EU jargon for the historic unifying of Europe. This ugly word was perhaps one reason why the policy never generated public enthusiasm. Another was – of course – the relentless anti-EU coverage in Britain's most influential newspapers. I saw this as my main challenge as I took over from Kim Darroch as head of news in August 2000.

Promotion was a surprise. 'They'll never let you have Kim's job,' the head of the government information service, Mike Grannatt, had told me. I was at 1CG with the Foreign Secretary one summer's evening for a conversation with two *Guardian* columnists, Martin Woolacott and Jonathan Steele. It was the kind of conversation Robin had earned the right to have, a serious overview of policy with none of the aggravations of personal and political difficulties. It was a measure of how well things were going that we could have this kind of session. Robin asked me to stay after the *Guardian* left, went upstairs to his flat and came back with a tray of various high quality bottled beers. After we had chosen, poured and sat back, he said: 'You're going to be head of news.'

He had done a deal with the Permanent Secretary, Sir John Kerr, on a series of moves resulting from a decision by Tony Blair to appoint our ambassador to Brussels, Sir Stephen Wall, as Number Ten advisor on the EU, a new post. This was part of an upgrading of the PM's foreign policy apparatus, with our NATO ambassador, Sir David Manning, going to Number Ten as advisor on non-EU foreign policy.

'Wall is going to be replaced by Sheinwald. Kim Darroch will replace Sheinwald as Director Europe. You will replace Kim.'

All these posts were to be filled formally by the Foreign Office board. Eventually Sherard rang to congratulate me that the board had appointed me Head of News. There was no Director of Communications at that time – the FCO judged the modest rank of Head sufficient for news. John Kerr informed me that he was now my line manager, but in practice I worked directly to the Foreign Secretary.

Promotion made two main differences to my working life. One was that I was running the press office rather than dealing only with specific issues and problems, now handling recruitment and other personnel issues, managing a team of 20 or so with a perpetual churn of young diplomats coming in with no experience of the media. This often worked, but not always. A new press officer on the Middle East who had never worked either on the media or the Middle East turned out to be very good. But in some cases bright young policy officials froze in the newsroom, losing their fluency and confidence in the face of the media, or when summoned at short notice by a minister. It was a regular frustration that press officers on two-year appointments would become competent in time to start applying for the next job. There was an attitude that people should be given the space in which to learn from mistakes. I wasn't prepared to have that.

Most press officers appreciated being guided away from mistakes, especially when on night duty, which could be a terrifying experience for them.

The other difference was that I now travelled with the Foreign Secretary always rather than occasionally. This would include four European summits a year. The first was to be in October at Biarritz: those were the days when the summits rotated from country to country. It was the French presidency: after Biarritz, Nice. I was looking forward to the travel but not to the summits. I had covered many as a political correspondent. They were enormous events, with hundreds of journalists packed into hot briefing rooms, where very senior people spoke quickly in jargon about numbingly complex negotiations. I wasn't sure I could pass myself off as a master of this arcane language and the policy nuances it seemed designed to conceal. I was naggingly worried that I wouldn't be able to manage, in a way that I never worried about any other aspect of foreign policy, for example the Middle East Peace Process. We travelled to Biarritz via Israel and the Palestinian Authority, but it was Biarritz rather than Jerusalem or Gaza that concerned me, though the Second Intifada – Palestinian uprising – had just begun and the situation was extremely tense.

We had dinner in Gaza City with Yassir Arafat, chairman of the PLO, and his team. Fish was served and Arafat was a typically generous Palestinian host, keen to serve us more and more. Robin was most un-keen, so I ate enough for him as well. We left for Jordan, to hear some dreadful news on arrival. Two Israeli soldiers had taken a wrong turning in Ramallah and been murdered. A picture of a Palestinian showing off his bloody hands to the crowd was a chilling symbol of the violence. The Foreign Secretary consulted the Prime Minister by phone and decided to go back to Chairman

Arafat to appeal for calm. We fetched up in the King David Hotel, Jerusalem, where the UN Secretary General, Kofi Annan, was staying. He and Robin had a discussion while officials rang Gaza to make arrangements. We had a chaotic, impromptu pavement press conference with Arafat long after midnight. I had not yet succeeded in getting Pat Barrie upgraded to travelling PA, though Yassir Arafat was in any case not one for orderly media events.

By the time we reached a rainy Biarritz, the summit was almost over, to my relief. Now for Nice, a much bigger event, which threatened to be one of the most difficult summits the EU had ever had. Bringing several new countries into the Union meant that every nation's voting weight had to be re-negotiated. This would be not only complex but politically sensitive. While it was arithmetically obvious that the more countries around the table, the less weight each must have relatively in voting, the eurosceptic media saw this as a weakening of British influence. In fact, the Prime Minister and Foreign Secretary had worked hard to build alliances with the newcomers, who appreciated Britain's role as 'champions of enlargement'. Britain could expect to have more allies, a better chance of forming blocking minorities against ideas we didn't like, and forging majorities for policies we wanted. But for the most strident of our newspapers Europe was a zero-sum relationship in which Britain must always lose. This had nothing to do with the complexities up for discussion at Nice, but was an ideological, even psychological problem with the whole idea of Britain as a European nation. Some in government had wearily accepted that no argument could be won on Europe, and that it was a waste of time to challenge the media to be serious about the intricacies of re-negotiated voting weights.

When it was all over, I wrote myself a note going back to

the start of the Foreign Secretary's preparations a few weeks before the summit, on a plane ride back from Greece. RAF flights home, with tea and scones, or dinner and wine, were always a good environment for thinking and planning and chatting, with no phones ringing:

> 'Robin said: 'I think we need a Europe media strategy'.
>
> I said: 'You have one in your box.'
>
> I had been thinking, more or less since the end of the holidays, that I should set out how to take on the Eurosceptic media and prevent them defeating us at the Nice summit. The year before, Robin and Tony Blair had returned from the Helsinki summit steaming with frustration at the way *The Sun, Mail* and others had dictated the media agenda, turning a successful summit into a media disaster. I wasn't going to let that happen again, and be blamed for it.
>
> More important, it has long seemed to me – I wrote this in the paper which Robin used as the basis for his post-Helsinki strategy submission to Blair – that the anti-European newspapers have set themselves the task of destroying this government's pro-European policy by making it impossible to speak up sensibly and moderately for Europe. Their propaganda is a poison which will, if not drawn, kill this country's commitment to Europe, within very few years.
>
> That is why we had at least to fight them to a draw at Nice. Had they won – by turning it into a 'defeat' as defined by their news values – it would have been a decisive and possibly fatal setback. I don't think it's exaggerating to say that Nice

was the last chance to stand up to them. We were perilously close to accepting once and for all that they couldn't be stood up to. There were moments, as Number Ten wobbled, when it looked as though defeat was being conceded by default. What Robin did at – and leading up to – Nice was to prove that the Eurosceptic media can be taken on and must be.

That is not to say they should be challenged head on, across the board. *The Sun* backed us over Sierra Leone [a brief military intervention to support the democratic government against its persistent rebels] and carried prominently a piece by Robin, defending our policy, which must have done him good with *The Sun's* 'patriotic' constituency.

I put 'patriotic' in inverted commas because this was the key word in the media strategy I had already drafted for Robin, when he raised the subject on the way back from Greece two months ago. The heart of the strategy was to challenge the sceptics for their monopoly on the patriotic case. What Robin liked in the paper I had written for him was the trio of sceptic phrases which I picked out for counter-attack: superstate, surrender, sovereignty. These have been the devastatingly simple basis of their assault on the Major and Blair governments.

Robin agreed that we should tackle this propaganda head-on, by making an issue of the Eurosceptic media's role, by reclaiming the 'national interest', by attacking the superstate myth, and by coming up with our own simple phrases to counter theirs. He liked my emphasis on using Europe to make Britain stronger. He asked me to do a core script, shift the Nice argument on to enlargement –

while finding a way of making enlargement sound
less dull. We agreed to stress the importance for
Britain of 20-odd democracies, bound together in
the world's biggest single market: stronger Britain
in a wider Europe.'

This phrase, a stronger Britain in a wider Europe, emerged
from a brainstorming session in the media team. We had
at that time an exceptionally gifted young press officer
for Europe, Mark Sedwill, a prime example of a brilliant
diplomat who had come in without any media experience,
and who took on the Europe file without any background in
it. As we tried to boil our argument down to something simple
– a soundbite, in trade jargon – I kept insisting that we must
focus on how enlargement would make Britain stronger: the
word 'stronger' being the key. Mark was grappling with how
to get away from the ugly word 'enlargement', talking about
'a wider Europe'. One or both of us at once said – a stronger
Britain in a wider Europe.

The soundbite culture of modern politics is often derided
as if political leaders could go on television or radio and
unfold their classical prose in leisurely fashion. It is the
media which has imposed soundbites, by exercising their
democratic right to interrupt, challenge, query, and catch you
out if you've said something slightly different to the words
used last week. Newspapers no longer carry long accounts
of parliamentary debates replete with chunks from speeches,
they have short headlines that are high on impact and low
on nuanced analysis: not just tabloids, but *The Times* and
Telegraph too.

Margaret Thatcher had coined the 'superstate' soundbite
in a seminal speech in Bruges in 1989, the first use of
the word that I know of, and certainly the moment when

it entered the political currency. In the following decade those who disputed this description of the European Union disdained to coin anything so simply powerful. I choose the word 'disdain' because I found a consistent reluctance among senior officials working on Europe (not all, but most of the most senior) to lower themselves to find arguments that might work with the public. I had a constant battle for clarity right through the Robin Cook and Jack Straw years, as if EU policy was far too complicated to make understandable outside a small group of very intelligent people in the Foreign Office and the office of the UK Representative in Brussels. In the preparations for Nice, there was a strong undertow of disbelief in the possibility of explaining these matters in plain language for real people. They had been through difficulties like the Maastricht Treaty of 1992, which had been savaged by many in the media and the Conservative Party, bringing John Major terrible difficulties of parliamentary survival, and they acted as though the press had shown itself to be unworthy of taking seriously. Tony Blair did take this challenge seriously, but his efforts to make a connection with the public on Europe were always belittled in private.

Sir Mark Sedwill, by the way, went on to be Ambassador to Afghanistan, Political Director of the Foreign Office, and then Permanent Secretary at the Home Office, a real star.

The internal discussions over Nice involved a three-way debate between myself; David Clark, Special Advisor on Europe; and Kim Darroch, recently promoted from Head of News to Director Europe. Kim and I got along very well as Head and Deputy of News, but he never agreed with my approach to explaining Europe, nor I with his. This was a difference of substance not just personality. I felt the language that Kim and his colleagues wrote in draft statements and speeches about Europe was too easy for *The Sun* to pillory, and so full of EU jargon that the public must be excluded from the debate; while Kim and some colleagues seemed always to feel that my drafts were too Eurosceptic, or glib, or not an accurate description of Europe's institutional arrangements. He was possibly right, but what wasn't right was to carry on with the usual way of doing things as if there were no problem. Kim refused to accept that there was a problem either with the government's relationship with the public on Europe, or with Britain's ability to maintain a positive role in Europe without public consent.

The third member of the triumvirate, David Clark, thought I was a touch eurosceptic, maybe a little too keen to avoid conflict with *The Sun*. This was an amicable difference of emphasis. We shared the same aim of trying to find new ways of reaching out beyond the converted to the non-political, newspaper-reading people on whose behalf government works. He wrote many of the best lines quoted below, from conviction, and reflecting with flair the Foreign Secretary's strong views.

'Apart from enlargement, Kim, David and I agreed on little else. Kim had gone so far as to write a counter-paper to my media strategy, casting doubt on several of my ideas. He had submitted it to Stephen Wall and side-copied to me, which I didn't find the most friendly act imaginable. At Robin's meeting, Kim argued that my whole approach was exaggerated, as we weren't in as much trouble as I thought – nowhere near as much as around the time of Maastricht. Of course, one of the problems with media strategy is that if you avoid the problem, people like Kim can argue the problem never existed. I argued that if we didn't do something soon we would wake up one morning and find that the eurosceptic media had made off with our Europe policy in the night; one day, perhaps soon, we would find that we had decisively lost public support for engagement with Europe. And we would never get it back. That was why we need a hard media strategy for Nice.

With David Clark, the disagreement was about the word 'nation'. I had been arguing for a while that we should be talking about 'a Europe of nations', that 'Europe's strength is its nations'. I had picked this up from listening to Robin talk about the impact of the new nations coming in through enlargement. I thought we need to be more explicit about this and had submitted some phrases of the sort for the Prime Minister's Warsaw speech in response to Fischer and Chirac [The German foreign minister and the French President had made speeches about their vision of Europe which pointed to a more integrated future than Britain wanted]. I was delighted that he [Blair] used a phrase Kim had tried to delete – that the European Union should act where the nations of Europe are stronger together than they can be alone; delighted too when he [Blair] took to referring to 'the Europe of nations'. David argued hard that the emphasis on nations was too sceptic. It smacked too much of the retreat Major had made from his 'heart of Europe' rhetoric. I strongly disagreed and still do. Unless you believe in a superstate, the nation has to be the basis of European Union, the guarantee of Europe's democracy and diversity.'

David and I came to an agreement on 'union of nations'. Robin later added 'union of democratic nations'. He agreed my core script in the back of his car, on the way from a visit to MI6 to lunch at the Financial Times. On that journey, he accepted my suggestion that he should use both his upcoming speeches, at the Centre for European Reform and at a Sheffield Star dinner, to launch and drive home the Nice media strategy. The FT asked for a piece trailing the speeches, which I pushed out to two or three other papers for the Monday morning. The intro was, from memory: 'It is time to reclaim the patriotic case for Europe' (Colin Crooks's – the new speech writer).'

Associated Press 13 November 2000
Robin Cook takes on the Eurospetics

Foreign Secretary Robin Cook today accused Eurosceptics of betraying their country, saying true patriots are fighting to secure Britain a leading place in the European Union.

"It is patriotism, it is national self-interest, to argue for Britain's full engagement as a leading partner in Europe," Cook said in a speech at the Center for European Reform.

"It is a betrayal of our nation and our future constantly to obstruct every fresh opportunity for co-operation in Europe."

Later today, Prime Minister Tony Blair was expected to take up the same theme in his annual address to bankers in the City. A draft of his speech released early to reporters indicated he would advocate "active and constructive engagement" with the other 14 members of the trading bloc.

Cook accused British sceptics and newspapers of peddling myths about Europe, including the suggestion that closer political and economic integration will lead to the creation of a controlling European "superstate."

"Euromyths provide great fun for journalists. The media has a mission to entertain, and some of them rise magnificently to that goal," Cook said. "But they are failing in their other mission – to inform.

"From now on, the government will be rebutting all such stories vigorously and promptly. You will be hearing the catchphrase 'facts, not myths' until that is the way the EU is reported."

Cook said the "biggest Euromyth of all" is the superstate claim, insisting that no EU member would allow this.'

My account of the Nice campaign continues:

'The government machine is nowhere near as efficient as you would imagine. It is fuelled by overwork, rather than by organisation. I had imagined that by submitting all my pieces of paper to Alastair Campbell, including one called "Europe: Trailing Next Week's Speeches", I had given clear notice of our intentions. And, since he had not protested, that Alastair had agreed. In fact, as he later said, Alastair saw neither piece of paper. I can only imagine that – like me, but only worse – he has so much paper flowing through his in tray that in the end he has to skim read too much. Mistakes are bound to be made. (I had also briefly mentioned to him that I was sending him a Europe media strategy, but we all have too many quick conversations in the midst of barely-controlled chaos).

Our mistake was to fail to flag up the significance of what we were doing at the Strategic Communications Unit.'

One of Alastair Campbell's improvements to government communication was to create a unit at Number Ten which co-ordinated all media activity through a weekly grid of events, to which all ministerial press offices had to submit their plans well enough in advance for discussion, amendment, delay, and sometimes veto. Alastair chaired a daily meeting at 8.30am to track media coverage against the grid and prepare responses to the unexpected or mishandled. I always tried to comply with this, seeing it as unprofessional to catch the Prime Minister and his media chief by surprise, not good for credibility. But on this occasion, while I had notified the unit, I had not done enough to flag the likely impact, although Alastair and I had discussed the general approach. Just as ministers do not always calculate their words as finely as the media assumes, so government media co-ordination is less coherent than supposed, because a few key people try to do too much.

The speech we had trailed was given by Robin Cook to the Centre for European Reform on 13 November 2000. It began:

> *'The sort of Europe I want to see in 2010 is a Europe with which everyone in this country can be comfortable. A wider Europe. A prosperous Europe. A safer Europe. A stable Europe. And a*

strong Europe.

A wider Europe because by 2010 we shall be well on the way to reuniting Europe. With up to a dozen new member states, the EU will have become the whole of the Continent, from the Arctic to the Mediterranean and from the Black Sea to the Atlantic. The Eurosceptics should reflect on why they want us to get off the bus when so many are queuing to get on.'

He got the euro out of the way early:

'I am not going to give the journalists their headlines for tomorrow morning by saying now whether I think Britain will be part of the Euro by then. It is astonishing how many acres of newsprint ministers can receive on the Euro by stating the obvious. Our policy is well-known, and we will continue to make the case for British membership. So let me put it this way: If the Euro is successful, if the economic tests have been met following our assessment early in the next Parliament, we will recommend entry to the British people in a referendum. And if the economic case is strong, I believe the British people will support entry.'

This was at the front end of agreed policy, not quite as neutral as the Chancellor's approach, in the assertion that Robin believed Britain would enter, but couched in terms too careful to make unwanted headlines.

'It is a delusion to imagine that Britain is stronger if it is isolated. The best way to project

> *British values and British interests is by doing so in partnership with those who share our values: democracy, human rights, justice and freedom....'*

The he took on the eurosceptic media – *The Sun, Mail, Telegraph, Express* – with scornful humour that echoed his style from his best performances in Opposition:

> *'Britain will reap the full benefits – security, prosperity and strength. Which makes it hard to fathom why so much of the discussion about Europe here – whether in the media, Parliament or political debates around the country – is dominated by fear and anxiety, not excitement. What sort of EU do parts of the British media foresee in 2010? An EU in which jackbooted Eurocops roam the streets of Britain, arresting anyone eating bent bananas or drinking beer in pints. A Europe where lollipop ladies are harmonised, where darts are banned from British pubs and where rubber ducks are banned from the great British bathtub. All of which, and more, have passed recently through the pages of our press....*
>
> *'Turning the tide of the national debate about Europe is about more than correcting error. We need to develop a positive storyline about Europe. This is not something the Government can or should be doing on its own. There are many national publications, and many journalists working for them, who do not share the ideological Euroscepticism of the Daily Mail. But, with the exception of the Financial Times, no newspaper in this country has a consistently objective narrative*

about Europe.

The biggest Euromyth of all is the myth of the superstate. There will not be a superstate because the British people would never allow it. And neither would the French people, the German people, the Italian people or the people of Poland, Hungary, Latvia or the other countries now queuing up to join the EU because they know it will make them stronger......

'Today I want to present the good news story that an objective press should be preparing to report from Nice next month. Many of them are already tipping their pens with doom and fear. But we should be looking forward to Nice with positive anticipation.....

It is a delusion of the Eurosceptics that a stronger Europe necessarily means a weaker Britain. On the contrary the stronger Europe is in the world the stronger will be Britain. A weak Europe means a weak Britain.....

I know which future I want for Britain. And I know that many in the press want that future too. It is time that all of us who share that vision of our future made sure that the British people can hear the positive reasons why they should choose a stronger Britain in a wider Europe.'

My note about the Nice campaign continues:

'The story of a hard-edged fightback on Europe ahead of Nice led the bulletins and spawned a month of coverage and commentary, which was exactly what I wanted. Number Ten was – shall we say – slow to come round to wanting it. I remember Godric Smith [Alastair's deputy] saying at Nice, when it was clear how well we had positioned ourselves – funny that we got where we are, when you think back to that difficult week we had. The beauty of the whole thing was that Alastair and I think similarly – Blair's speech at Mansion House [mentioned in the AP report above] was about enlightened patriotism. But, on Europe, he is tactically more cautious.

Alastair said he felt we were saying the right things, but too over-the-top. Clearly we were going to have trouble with the second speech on the Thursday. It wasn't that our message had gone wrong, simply that we were pushing other news aside. Alastair and Blair are currently having a big crackdown on ministers who upstage the grid. When we notified Number Ten that we intended to trail the Thursday speech on the Today programme, word came back from Alastair via Tim Livesey [Number Ten press officer for foreign issues] that this would push Prescott's housing initiative off the top of the grid on a day when Cabinet would be discussing the need to stop upstaging the grid: this would not be good for Robin, especially in his absence. We were in Marseilles, for a Euromed summit.

Robin was at the dinner. I waited up to give him this happy news. He refused to take it. As it was very late and Alastair would have gone to bed, he decided not to wake him and argue but do the [*Today*] programme anyway. Just after Robin had gone to bed, we heard that Peter Mandelson had given the *FT* a story pushing at the edges of euro policy, as he does from time to time. This would be bound to dominate the *Today* interview. I went and knocked up Robin to ask him if he was absolutely sure. He was in pyjamas. He invited me in, listened, told me to stop worrying and get to bed.

I wasn't well. By morning my voice had gone. So I briefed Robin for this exceptionally difficult interview in whispers. John Humphrys was completely uninterested in Robin's speech that night, only in trying to lead him into the traps set by Mandelson's euro intervention.

We got strong word back via private office that Jonathan Powell [PM's chief of staff] and John Sawers [private secretary for foreign affairs at Number Ten] did not want us publicising the Sheffield speech.

After doing the Today programme, Robin produced several vitamin C tablets and said: 'Take those and have a lie down'. Before I got to bed, I had a call from the *Telegraph* asking for a leader page piece from Robin – Charles Moore [editor] was intrigued that someone was at last saying there was a positive case and, though he doubted that one existed, he wanted Robin to try to explain it. This was too good to resist.

I gave up the idea of bed and walked up to the conference centre, where I found Robin in one of those moments when there just isn't enough time to do everything. Tim [Barrow, private secretary for EU issues] was in the process of telling him that Number Ten wanted us keeping a low profile on Europe, but that Blair wanted Robin to speak second after Brown at the next day's election strategy Cabinet.

When I mentioned the *Telegraph* offer Robin said of course we should do it, but he wouldn't have time. I'd have to make sure it was right.

It needed to be strong enough to make the paper, but not so strong as to upset Number Ten. It needed to be positive, but cool, patriotic, but calm. And, the big tactical judgement, it needed to say out loud that majority voting was good for Britain, in the right circumstances. Majority voting (QMV) was one of the main Nice problems. Clearly there were going to be many items moved from unanimous decision-making . Once the sceps made QMV the big issue at Nice, we would be in trouble. We had to try to neutralise the issue, but doing so risked making it the issue.The *Telegraph* piece worked beautifully. George Jones [political editor] picked out the QMV passage for his front page piece, but because we had given the *Telegraph* quite a big exclusive they were on their best behaviour and treated the subject fairly. I wouldn't have predicted this, but, although we had some awkward moments on it, QMV was never again a problem.'

Here is the *Telegraph* piece in full:

BRITAIN'S approach to next month's Nice Summit will be confident, patriotic and pro-European. I see no contradiction in putting the words "patriotic" and "pro-European" alongside each other.

I understand that not everyone in Britain sees Europe in this way. There are few more reasoned and articulate exponents of the Euro-sceptic position than Charles Moore, the Editor of The Daily Telegraph, and I am grateful for this chance to put my side of the story to his readers today.

Many Telegraph readers share Mr Moore's view that the Euro-sceptic argument is based on the national interest. I respect that. And I would ask you to respect the fact that our pro-European argument is also based on the national interest. It is a pity that much Euro-sceptic commentary assumes that engagement in Europe is against the national interest, as if any negotiated agreement with our European partners must by definition be made at the expense of Britain.

I have set out this week to try to reclaim the patriotic ground from our Euro-sceptic critics. No one should think it strange to say that we are at the same time patriotic and pro-European. Last night in Sheffield I set out three British principles on which we pursue our national interest within the EU:

• a strong Europe means a strong Britain;

• Europe is a union of democratic nations;

• we achieve more for Britain by playing a leading role than by standing on the sidelines.

After more than three years of working, week in, week out, with our European partners, I am convinced that full engagement is a better way for Britain to look after its national interests than isolation. Everyone is familiar with the club bore who does nothing but complain, never making any constructive contribution. Nobody listens to the club bore. That is the isolated role that I believe would be bad for Britain in Europe. Europe will always be our biggest market. Developments in the EU affect our lives whether we are engaged or not. I would far rather be helping to set the rules and playing an active role. Britain needs a strong Europe and Europe needs strong nations. The point of the Nice Summit is not to undermine British sovereignty, but to build a wider Europe in which Britain will be stronger and more prosperous. We want to reunite the established democracies of western Europe with the re-emerging democracies in the east. Nice is about reforming Europe in readiness for this rebellion. It is self-evident that this is in Britain's interests. It should be equally self-evident that we must play a leading role in negotiating the treaty that makes it possible. We must dispel the myths. The myth is that Nice is about taking power away from Britain. The fact is that it is about building a stronger Britain in a wider Europe. Europe makes us stronger because 15 or more nations together are better able to fight cross-border crime, drugs, pollution and unemployment. The myth is that European defence will cut across Nato's functions. The fact is that Nato is and will remain the sole basis of our territorial defence. The EU will act only in response to crises and where Nato as a whole is not engaged. European Security and Defence Policy enhances the armoury at our disposal and that is why the US administration and military establishment have welcomed it. The biggest myth about Europe is the superstate. That is why the second of our British principles describes the EU as a union of democratic nations. The fact is that the national identities, cultures and traditions of the democratic nations of Europe are too strong to be subsumed. The EU is unique in world history. No other nations have done so much to pool their strength in the common interest while retaining the sovereignty and identity that make them distinct and diverse. As my French counterpart, Hubert Vedrine, expresses it, Britain and France will never agree to the status of a Massachusetts or a Virginia. Tony Blair and I aren't going to Nice to negotiate a superstate. It is not on the agenda. We are going there to work for more votes for Britain in the European Council.

To argue for majority voting where this can promote the national interest and to maintain the veto where it protects the national interest. Many myths surround majority voting. To read some commentators, you would think that it had just been invented. In fact, 80 per cent of decisions are already taken by majority voting. And Britain is usually on the winning side. Of 85 votes in the past two calendar years, Britain was in the majority 80 times. That means there were 80 decisions in Britain's interest, which others could have blocked if the decision had been subject to veto. France and Germany were outvoted more often than Britain. "Britain isolated" is an outdated caricature. At Nice, we will insist that majority voting is not extended into areas where we need the veto to protect the national interest, including tax and social security. We have made clear that, in these and other areas, we have red lines. Others will go to Nice with red lines of their own. All 15 countries will be negotiating in their national interest. This is not a case of Britain isolated, but of Britain standing up for our interests, as all our partners do. But where, case by case, we believe we can promote the national interest by majority voting, we will agree to it. We have achieved much over the years for Britain through majority voting. Directives on banking and insurance that helped the City were opposed by other countries, which would have blocked them if they had had a veto. Our aim at Nice is a more prosperous and secure Britain, at home in a reunited Europe. We will argue our case with confidence, because we believe there is no reason why things that are distinctly British should be threatened by a bustling, successful, prosperous Europe in which Britain is a leading partner.

My note continues:

'I was supposed to go to Sheffield with Robin, from Marseilles, but my voice was gone and my energy with it. I came home and tried to get a long weekend off. But on the Saturday night, I had a call from the *Observer* asking me to explain the *Sunday Telegraph* splash claiming that Robin had authorised a spokesman to attack Gordon Brown for interfering on Europe, telling him – you're not Prime Minister yet [Get your tanks off our lawn, says Cook' – the headline, from memory]. While trying to raise Robin, I checked with David Clark, who didn't completely deny having spoken to Joe Murphy [Sunday Telegraph political editor]. Robin confirmed that he had not broken with the habit of a lifetime, nobody had been authorised, those were not his views and how did I propose to kill the story, within the next ten minutes? This was hard as both of us had a nasty feeling it would turn out that David Clark had indeed spoken loosely. I assured all the Sundays – my voice was returning – that no such comments had been authorised.

Eveyone knew what had happened. I pointed out to David that he should think a bit before speaking. It's damaging Robin and we can't have it happen again. This is the last time anyone will believe it's unauthorised. I told both Robin and David that I have burned all my credibility persuading people it's unauthorised.

I'm convinced Robin does disapprove of this stuff and knows it's self-defeating. But why doesn't he stop it? I have believed until now that he doesn't stop it because he's too lenient and too loyal. He can't be a control freak. I will go on believing that a bit longer, but we've reached the stage where not stopping it is in effect a positive act. I'm very much afraid it's going to undo the good work we have done in re-building Robin as a serious, solid, trustworthy, thoroughly competent Cabinet heavyweight. There's a limit to how much I can do.

I'm having a lot of trouble on this front, and with officials who speak freely to the media under disguise of 'senior sources', etc. Just before Nice, there were a couple of stories in the *FT* in quick succession, which Number Ten thought had been placed with Andy Parker [political correspondent] by someone at the FCO briefing against Downing Street. I was a prime suspect, though I know that only by luck and thanks to Pat's loyalty. One afternoon while I was out, Alastair's secretary rang and said they had sent me an e-mail by mistake – could she destroy it and not tell me about it? They thought they were dealing with the secretary I had inherited from Kim, not realising Pat was also working with me. Pat made sure I saw it first. They'd meant to send me a note from Alastair telling me to find out who is leaking and put a stop to it. What they actually sent me was the note from Sawers to Campbell 'to read the riot act to Williams'.

I rang Alastair and, without giving Pat away, said I hoped his message to me didn't imply that I was under suspicion. I believe Alastair's assurance that he knows I don't brief against Number Ten, or anyone else, because he knows what a tight game I've played since coming to work for Robin. I'm convinced too that he thinks Robin is straight. Sawers' note made clear that Kerr is casting doubt on my straightness. As I said to him [John Kerr] – I asked for an immediate meeting – if Number Ten doubts my straightness my usefulness to Robin and the FCO is reduced by about 70 per cent. On Robin's advice – I had a quiet chat with him at 1CG after doing a Saturday night pre-record – I approached Kerr as if I assumed his faith in my honesty and wanted his help in straightening things out.

I also asked Alastair to put Sawers straight for me. He said he would. I spoke to Peter Hain – also named as a suspect in the note – who protested to Sawers. Later that morning I was at a Cabinet Office meeting on Europe. Sawers sent me a note of apology across the table. [John Sawers became Political Director of the FCO in Jack Straw's time and we had a superb working relationship, especially during the launch of the long-running nuclear negotiations with Iran. As Sir John, he become UK representative to the United Nations and then C, head of M16.]

None of this solved either of the problems – loose-talking officials and loose-talking political people. Kerr and I agreed that we would have a leak inquiry the next time something happened. We did. Someone talked freely to the BBC about Robin and Peter's misgivings on National Missile Defence – bonehead tactics as a Republican administration takes over. [This was a US plan to provide a supposedly defensive shield which many, including Robin, thought provocative to Russia, rather than defensive]. This is the trouble with people who talk loosely to the media. They are all terribly clever, with a wonderful grasp of policy, but not an ounce of common sense. How can it help to paint Robin into a corner on an issue as large and dangerous as NMD? And if anyone's going to do the painting, shouldn't it be Robin himself, deliberately?

> This is a long way from Europe, except that
> media discipline is more important on Europe than
> on anything."

Another learning point in my transition from journalist to spokesman was that news stories attributed to 'a senior source' or 'a source close to', are not always part of a clever plan. And if they cause difficulties, nobody owns up. I am conscious that deploring this in my notes at the time makes me seem a caricature control-freak media person. But there is a serious point, that in our democratic system it is the elected minister who answers for policy in parliament, so he or she is entitled to have some control, through the press office, over what is said on the ministry's behalf, on or off the record.

My view in retrospect is that there is a balance to be struck, and I think I got better at striking it as I gained experience. John Sawers was a very good example of a 'senior source' who briefed the media off the record about complex negotiations, like Iran. I encouraged this, and the more often I encouraged him and other big figures in the office to talk to serious correspondents, the better it was for all parties. The media got detailed briefing direct from the person engaged in the talks, I knew on the Foreign Secretary's behalf that our policy was being professionally articulated by the expert, sometimes exerting influence on the country across the negotiating table, and the media felt it was getting solid information, not a line to take. And the public was being well informed.

What is not right, in my view, is an unelected official speculating about ministerial policy without the minister knowing about it, directly or through the press office. If a minister chooses to challenge government policy, question strategy or influence decisions in the making by briefing the media, it is for him or her to weigh the risk, the propriety and the wisdom, or to delegate the judgement to a professional spokesperson in whom the Secretary of State has confidence. My note continues:

'Our contribution to the Nice strategy was to hold a series of exhaustive media briefings. We targeted the lobby, because it's the lobby that turns up ignorantly at European Councils (I've done it too) and decides what the story is. The Brussels correspondents get the second byline and don't direct the story. We had to educate the lobby, soak them in our strategy, woo them and win them over, flatter them and stroke them and make them feel we were helping them get the story right. It worked. But both Alastair and Kim argued for concentrating on the Brussels corrs. Robin and I ploughed on. My old friends in the lobby say now that our strategy was absolutely right, because they just couldn't fall for the usual superstate stuff having been given so much briefing on what Nice was really about.

Having found ourselves working semi-accidentally towards the same end by similar means, Alastair decided to convene a meeting with me, Stephen Wall [PM's senior advisor on Europe] and others. I went with Kim and James Bevan, the media-savvy Head of the FCO's European Union department. Sawers turned up half way through. Alastair was all for targeting the Brussels corrs, and was full of ideas like getting leaders of the accession countries to say how damaging it would be if the summit failed. (We delivered on the latter with our opening-day press conference with, among others, Tomas Ilves of Estonia, whom the lobby spotted as an anagram of Elvis. We did our own number with the Brussels corrs on the final Monday). I argued that, however useful this all was, the real target had to be the lobby. It was nice to have the lobby – George Jones, Andy Grice [*Independent*] – saying afterwards that this tactic was absolutely right. It was also absolutely risky and difficult.

Robin played the lobby beautifully. They respect and like him and know him for what he is, a class act. The lobby decides not only what the story is at summits, but what the story is on the politics of personality – who's up, who's down, who's in and who's going out. His survival – anyone's survival – depends critically on opinion in the lobby.

We were frank with everyone that our briefing blitz was a deliberate attempt to do things differently – as John Sargeant said, trust us with the facts. We had Sargeant and Adam Boulton [Sky] in twice, in order to draw the broadcasters away from the agenda set by Trevor Kavanagh [political editor of *The Sun*].

We tried to avoid a numbers game and knew we couldn't afford to let that be the yardstick by which Nice was judged. But neither could we prevent the media doing it. At the main pre-Nice lobby briefing, Robin said he thought the end result 'likely to be nearer a third than a half' of the 50 articles the presidency had tabled for discussion. As he also joked that Trevor had 'made a surprisingly modest guess at 17', they all took 17 as our prediction and all used it next day. The Maastricht record was 30 articles moved to QMV, and we thought that 17 wasn't a bad estimate – the only question was whether it was good tactics to surface it. It was only after that episode with the lobby that Kim started to say the figure was going to be much higher than we had thought, saying it as if we should have known that.'

This passage is a reminder of how tediously complicated the Nice agenda was if you bogged down in detail. QMV was jargon for qualified majority voting, that is, the system by which every country in the EU has a weight allotted to its vote, relative to its size. This is to avoid, say, Malta and Cyprus outvoting Germany. But it is not a straight mathematical relationship between population and voting weight; otherwise the smallest countries would have insignificant voting power. The weighting was a matter of negotiation. There was going to have to be haggling at Nice over how we all adjusted our voting strengths to accommodate countries as varied in size as Poland and Latvia. In this haggling, we were going to have to be very careful about where we came out relative to existing partners.

The references to 'articles being moved to QMV' mean items of EU policy which could be decided by a majority vote: that is, with no-one having a veto. The Eurosceptic media regarded any loss of veto power – any article 'moved to QMV' – as a loss for Britain. This was why we had concentrated so hard on re-framing the argument to make clear that there were many articles on which we were happy to do away with the veto, but a few which were 'red lines'.

'Actually, our alleged 17 was high enough to prepare the ground for major movement, but not so high as to set off a media screaming fit. *The Times*, for instance, was intrigued by the idea that we wanted many of these articles moved to QMV and did a good job of explaining why. Thus by the time we got to Nice, the media had well and truly accepted the fact that the total wasn't the key fact, as so many of these articles were either desirable, trivial or not deal-breakers. The deal-breakers – tax, social security etc – were clear enough to stay in their minds. And the pressure put on by the presidency was not intense because Blair and Cook had signalled so clearly and consistently that we were not giving way. As Robin said in his final-week soundbite – we have been clear, consistent and constructive – three Cs. (Mark Sedwill did a very good send-up of Williams core-scripting, which consisted entirely of a list of numbers: 3 Cs, four key principles, six red lines, etc)

In the end more than 30 articles were moved to QMV. There still isn't a definitive number.'

We needed to make the argument over Europe a debate about national strategy rather than a squabble over tactical issues. It is often a problem in foreign policy that the wide-angled strategy – why something matters to the country and the world – is lost in the detailed disputes. This has been one of the fundamental weaknesses of the pro-European case, that the strategic advantage is rarely articulated, allowing the media to focus the public on aggravatingly obscure and menacing little problems, which matter, but which should not be the definition of British strategy. Once you are stuck in arguments over close-focus problems like how many articles will be moved from unanimous decision-making to majority voting, you are bound to be on the defensive. And if you defend yourself in jargon – like QMV, qualified majority voting – you sound obsessed with things far removed from people's daily concerns.'

There were no accusations of Robin failing to do his homework, leading up to Nice. He had his confidence back and was dealing with something that suited his skills: the brain power to get right on top of the detail and the articulacy that came from really believing in what he was doing. It involved close working with the Prime Minister. Tony Blair valued Robin's relish for detail. That is not to suggest that Blair didn't grasp it too, but it must be a very uneasy feeling, playing a many-sided game of chess at an EU negotiation, live, without the chance to call in advice, or to go back and start again if you find you're in difficulty. So it must be a comfort to a Prime Minister to have confidence in his Foreign Secretary.

We were now only a few months short of the election expected in 2001. Robin increasingly had in mind that reshuffle that would follow Blair's expected second victory. A successful EU negotiation would be the perfect lead-in. A failure, of course, wouldn't. It was one of the longest and most difficult of all EU summits.

> 'The working environment at these events is very peculiar. Basically, you spend hours lolling about with little to do, and minutes working intensely hard.
>
> My working day would start early with the cuttings, a short preparation session with Robin to agree the key message to get across for the day – his morning media run had to set the news agenda for a day in which he would have few if any media opportunities. We would do this in the private office downstairs in the seafront hotel, with Robin doing Today, etc on the phone.
>
> He and I would then go to breakfast with the FCO team [Kerr, Kim etc] to prepare for that day's serious bargaining. Robin raced through the key passages,

not so much asking for advice as leading his senior officials through the text, letting them make points of fact and offer pieces of advice. He had at least as good a grasp of the detail as any of the experts. He was also shrewd in his suggestions for tactical negotiating gambits for the Prime Minister.'

The epic negotiation lasted five days as Jacques Chirac was determined to settle the issue under his Presidency, and applied a familiar EU tactic of forcing decisions through sheer exhaustion, though taking it to unusual lengths. Only the PM and Foreign Secretary are 'in the room', while officials of the many countries work in crowded offices with not enough chairs, seizing notes written by your country's one official allowed to sit in an ante-room listening to the discussion and summarising it. It is a desperately inefficient way of doing serious international business. The Anticis, as they are known (even note takers have jargon attached to them in the EU) are not chosen for their shorthand, as they have none, nor are they particularly senior, though they are very bright. Officials have no means of feeding advice back into 'the room', and anyway are always behind the action as it takes time for the Antici notes to come round the delegation rooms.

So at EU summits, the Prime Minister and Foreign Secretary are unusually intimate and isolated, one of the reasons why they have to have a good working relationship. The Blair-Cook partnership was a good mix of strengths. Some officials exaggerated the PM's tendency to deal in the big shapes of foreign policy, as if he could do that without grasping the essentials among the detail. Tony Blair appreciated Robin Cook's forensic skills, as displayed in Opposition on the Scott Report. It would be an exaggeration as well to portray Robin as only a details man. In a big negotiation, the key is to know which details matter most and how they fit together in a pattern that either delivers your objectives, or gives the initiative to others. Most around the table at Nice had no interest in Britain's neuralgic sensitivity to supposed threats to national sovereignty, nor any grasp of how QMV was potentially very painful, if Tony Blair were to 'surrender' too much. And the chairman of the summit, Jacques Chirac, was not a neutral arbiter of discussion, but a shrewd operator of very long experience who enjoyed British discomfort. It was said of a British admiral during World War One that he could have lost the war in the course of an afternoon, but didn't. The same is true at European summits. Alone, without official support and advice, the Prime Minister and Foreign Secretary might easily lose an argument of huge long-term significance, during the course of the night, when horribly tired.

> 'Suddenly around 4.30am it was over and we went across to the media centre for the Blair/ Cook press conference. It was a marvel of stamina to do it. It gave me enormous pleasure to hear Robin speaking the core script – stronger Britain, wider Europe – and to hear it sounding so right when measured against the outcome. Not that the outcome was precisely clear.
>
> Alastair whispered: "When we leave, who's staying behind to explain the deal?"
>
> I said: "What precisely is the deal?"
>
> "I don't know. Only those two up there know."
>
> I found Sawers and whispered: "What is the new QMV threshold?"
>
> Sawers looked at the agreed table, much scrawled on and crossed-out, and whispered back: "I don't know."'

The point of the QMV threshold was that Robin had told the Commons we would not settle for less than Britain being able to form a blocking minority with a handful of allies – 'bigs' and 'smalls' as the varied nations of Europe were referred to. We couldn't afford to find ourselves relying too heavily on getting 'big' allies as that would give France and Germany scope to join forces and leave us to scrabble for votes among the 'smalls'. As long as the threshold for a qualified majority was set far enough above 50%, we could be confident of defending our interests. Our target was to get the threshold a couple of points above 60%, with our own share of the vote calculated not too far behind the biggest country, Germany. At one breakfast, I had added up the percentages in the draft and raised the alarm that we were short of Robin's pledge. The final agreement met our threshold – my small arithmetic contribution to EU history.

> 'In fact, there was a bust-up among EU ambassadors back in Brussels the following week when they realised it wasn't clear to anyone what had been agreed. They eventually put together an agreement that reflects our understanding of what Blair and Cook thought they had achieved – in an enlarged union, Britain will be able to form a blocking minority with any two other 'bigs'. That had been our bottom line.
>
> At our lobby briefing we had handed out a list of eight aims, which I had knocked off hurriedly. Robin said Andy Grice [*The Independent*] told him we had achieved seven and a half. I made it eight.
>
> Robin came out the big winner. It was very obvious how important he is to Blair in these hard, detailed negotiations. The weekend after Nice Andy Grice ran a piece saying Robin is likely to

stay at the FCO beyond the election, having 'played a blinder at Nice', according to a senior source.

This is an extraordinary turnaround. We're not there yet. But Pam bought me Andrew Rawnsley's book [*Servants of the People*] for Christmas and it reminded me of just how far we have come from the time when Robin could plausibly be described by a serious commentator as 'cackhanded'.

There is still a huge amount to do – the European defence initiative is unravelling. And we still have our ever-present problem 'senior source' and 'one official' saying whatever comes into their clever heads.'

For the record, before Nice, the voting weights among the EU of 12 added up to 87, of which Germany, France, Italy and the UK had 10 each, Spain 8. The result of the Nice negotiation was that in the EU of 27, there would be a total of 258 votes, of which Germany, France, Italy and the UK would have 29 each, Spain and Poland 27. The threshold for a majority was 62%, or 207 of the 258 votes. This meant that, to block a proposal that ran against UK interests, we would still only need the support of one other large Member State (such as Germany or Poland) to reach 52 votes needed for a blocking minority. Or we could find those 52 votes through a combination such as Britain (29) plus Belgium (12), Sweden (10) and Lithuania (7). So amid all these numbers, the UK had achieved its aim of protecting our national interests.

Nine

Indispensible? Or Takeaway?

N one of us was going to become complacent, but I knew it had been Alastair Campbell briefing that Robin was going to remain Foreign Secretary beyond the election. Despite Alastair's 'hate them' remarks a few months earlier, he had mature working relationships with long-serving political editors like Andy Grice of *The Independent* and Phil Webster of *The Times*. If they and some others ran this kind of piece, it was well-founded. Phil Webster wrote that Jack Straw was being lined up as the next Foreign Secretary, but not until midway through the next parliament, so clearly the Prime Minister and his spokesman wanted Robin Cook to feel secure after his long anxiety. Midway through the next parliament would take Robin to six years, meeting his ambition to overtake Ernie Bevin as the longest-serving Labour Foreign Secretary.

If so, he was going to have to work with a new right-wing administration in the United States. Bill Clinton had been much admired by and close to Tony Blair as a fellow centre-left leader with the emphasis very much on centre. When Clinton reached the end of his second term, his vice-president Al Gore ran against George W Bush. Robin and I were waiting for the results at 1CG with a radio car outside on the morning after the election in early November, so that the Foreign Secretary could say something diplomatic about the result either way. Usually US election results are clear well before Britain gets up in the morning, but this one was very close. At a few minutes to eight, we were told that Gore had conceded defeat. Bush – further right than his father, the previous President – was not going to be a comfortable ideological match, but Robin managed to welcome the result without hypocrisy, trying out the sort of bland transatlantic mutual respect that was now going to have to be routine. He had been tentatively developing a relationship with Colin Powell, who was marked out as the likely Secretary of State in a Republican administration, and was interested in working alongside this much more subtle, centrist figure than Bush himself.

I was walking back across St James' Park to the office when I took a call from Charles Reiss, political editor of The *Evening Standard*, who had been my boss for many years. He said there was a slight problem with what Robin had just been saying. I thought I must have missed some policy nuance that Robin had slightly mis-spoken, but it was more serious than that. 'Gore has un-conceded,' said Charles. This was the beginning of the saga of the hanging chads of Florida, which delayed a result for weeks. It would have been a touch awkward had Robin had to go back on air later to welcome Gore, having welcomed Bush. It is the only time I know of that a Presidential candidate has conceded and then un-conceded, and it happened to happen either side of the Today programme's prime slot at ten past eight in the morning.

One of the first visits of the New Year was to Washington to open working relations. Powell was a joy – I was to see a lot of him later, in Jack Straw's time – but Vice-President Dick Cheney, possibly as far to the right as anyone who ever held high office anywhere, eyed the visiting socialist coldly, said as few words as possible, and ended the meeting as quickly as he could. As I noted: 'He was just listening, as if Robin had to prove himself. I've never been in a meeting with someone so rude.'

I have wondered what would have happened if Robin had remained Foreign Secretary as apparently intended at that time, through the terrorist attack on America that was a few months away, into the period of Bush-Cheney's move towards war in Iraq. Obviously he would have resigned, though with much greater impact as Foreign Secretary than as Leader of the Commons. Given the parliamentary peril Tony Blair was in as war approached, Robin must have either brought the government down or presented such a threat that Blair would have backed away. I can't imagine the latter. So the final months of Robin's time as Foreign Secretary, from his triumph at Nice in December, to the reshuffle in June, are a fascinating time, with hindsight, given what might have been if Tony Blair had stuck with his signalled intention around the end of 2000 to keep Robin at the FCO. Something changed. I can't be sure what. Robin's fate may have been decided while Cheney eyed him up as a pinko. Or maybe he was the victim of a reshuffle jigsaw that didn't quite fit on the day. My notes provide some clues to this who-done-it; or rather why-done-it, since the question is why Tony Blair changed his mind, and accidentally – I presume – avoided a possibly fatal collision with his Foreign Secretary on the eve of the Iraq war.

'Saturday, 10 February, 2001.
A memorable week, starting in Washington and finishing with a talk to the Prime Minister in the lovely little French town, Cahors. First, the background. Peter Mandelson resigned a couple

of weeks ago and is now fighting back, presenting himself as the victim of a kangaroo court consisting of his old friends Blair and Campbell.

There's a new Republican administration in Washington with a hawkish defence policy and no ideological reason to befriend the Blair government. So Robin went to make the first contacts, knowing that – as with Nice – this could be a disaster, but could on the other hand show him as a substantial international figure.

As Peter Riddell said in *The Times*, the visit would be as much about news management as about policy. It had to look right. We built up in similar fashion to Nice, briefing the right people heavily around a core script – closest ally, establishing personal rapport, stronger in Europe, stronger in Washington. I also wrote a core script on national missile defence – the most dangerously divisive issue. Robin agreed to given an interview to Peter and Phil Webster. To my dismay, they led him off script and into the euro. I had warned him they would. He didn't say anything at odds with policy, but the length and warmth of his comments was clearly a story, especially in the wake of Mandelson's departure – the media is speculating about the possible shift of balance in Cabinet away from the euro and towards Brown's position. When I told Robin he'd given them a good euro story, he was bemused and appalled. 'If I go out on a limb on the euro now, I won't be foreign secretary after the election.'

I spent the weekend negotiating with Phil, but

The Times led with the euro comments (carefully written, to Phil's credit), using a flattering piece on Robin/US inside.'

We left for America on Monday lunchtime.

'Sherard and I shared a car to Heathrow. On the plane, I wrote a paper for Robin on how to play the next steps on Europe. We drove into Washington in late afternoon sunshine, a gloriously clear winter's day. I was staying at the residence.

At the State Department, Colin Powell made a big fuss of Robin. He's a nice man, with a big genuine smile, who laughs a lot. He struck me as having a good grip and a clear sense of priorities. But Sherard and Meyer [Sir Christopher Meyer, ambassador to Washington and a former head of news] thought him a second rate intellect. Emyr [Jones Parry, Political Director of the FCO] disagreed, and thought him intellectually more impressive than Albright. Sherard, it has to be said, is an awful snob. I'll take a punt on Powell emerging as the major figure of the next decade, a man impossible to classify, with the creative ability to focus on what matters and surprise the world with his originality.

I very much hope Robin can work with him for a decent length of time, because they would make a marvellous partnership, if I'm right about Powell. Already, that partnership is well under way. Powell's analysis of Iraq was uncannily like Robin's.'

It is tantalising that I took for granted in this note – and so didn't explain – what this shared analysis was. I will not try to think backwards on Iraq of all subjects. But it is an interesting point that in early 2001, there was no divergence between Robin Cook and the US Secretary of State. Obviously this was before the sequence of events which resulted in war. There was no hint at this stage, as far as I recollect, of the new US administration moving towards war,

And it is tantalising as well to think what a force for good Colin Powell might have been had he not been increasingly sidelined by Dick Cheney and the equally hawkish Defense Secretary Donald Rumsfeld. My judgement of Powell's future was way off. It was hard to imagine so substantial a figure being outmanouevred by men as unimpressive as Cheney and Rumsfeld, but he was.

> 'We had lunch – huge lamb chops – in a wood panelled dining room with a big American flag fluttering outside the window and a view of the Potomac. At the end, Powell asked Richard Boucher [State spokesman] and me to brief him and Robin on the press conference. Boucher took them through what was running in the media. I just said to Powell (Robin was well-rehearsed by then): 'What the British media is looking for is any nuance between you, especially on defence.' They were beautiful together, a real double act. Boucher and I took it in turn to call questioners and the best sign of success was when British hands stopped going up – they knew they were getting no nuances. As they came off the platform, Robin said to Powell: 'Look, my press officer is smiling. He doesn't often do that.'

Despite this outcome, on the journey back to London, Sherard Cowper-Coles said to me: 'The strain on you must be enormous. You mustn't let it affect your health or sanity'. I noted at the time that I was 'panned out', and complained to myself about 'office politics', in particular about Sir John Kerr, the Permanent Secretary. The relevant point to this account is not my relationship with him, but Robin Cook's. Kerr was a brilliant diplomat, who had given legendary service to Margaret Thatcher during her battles in Europe. It was alleged that he had hidden himself under the table during a negotiation and passed notes up to her. He cultivated a reputation for being wickedly cunning. It took me a while to realise he was not entirely enthusiastic about my presence. This was of no consequence compared with his lack of enthusiasm for the Foreign Secretary, which was reciprocated. One problem was that both John Kerr and Robin Cook had long been used to being the cleverest person in the room – any room – so there wasn't space for both intellects, without friction. I remember a sadly un-noted winter's afternoon at Chevening when Robin asked me down for a good, long, reflective talk, after he had dealt with office business with his Permanent Secretary. Kerr stayed on, to Robin's mounting irritation. Their mutual dislike was like a warm fire in the room.

This was not just about competing intellects at the top of the range, nor only a matter of spiky personalities. Robin felt Sandline had revealed the office to be a managerial shambles, while John Kerr made only a slight effort to disguise his contempt for Robin's working methods. It is a very great pity that these two outstandingly gifted individuals subtracted from rather than strengthened one another.

Both suffered for their mutual inability to work together. When I first arrived, as deputy head of news, the Sandline controversy was crumpling both their reputations. John Kerr was glad of my advice on how to deal with select committee hearings so that he anticipated embarrassing questions and didn't have to 'check his memory' and correct his evidence, as he had damagingly had to do when the controversy had first broken. He expressed appreciation when his subsequent brushes with parliamentary inquiries passed off without trouble, paying a nice compliment in evidence to the Standard and Privileges Committee inquiry into the Ernie Ross leak. When I thanked him, he said: 'I meant it.'

John Kerr asked me at one stage to help repair his relationship with the Foreign Secretary. This proved beyond me, though I tried. I suggested that the Permanent Secretary accompany the Foreign Secretary on a big foreign visit – Moscow and Murmansk – but he said that wasn't his role, which had been my point: do something unusual to build their relationship.

Things changed after I was promoted from deputy to head of news, useful problem-solver to the chief spokesman and media advisor. I can understand that this must have been a blow to FCO managerial pride, having a hack take a job that I had heard described as 'one of the mid-career Crown Jewels'. Most of the Office managed to take this blow with good grace and many welcomed the sharper edge with which the Foreign Office was dealing with the media, anticipating more and reacting less.

For John Kerr, I suppose I was something of a proxy for Robin. Kerr could accuse me of poor management – as he did – when he couldn't accuse Robin. I never pointed out the irony of being lectured about management, having come in during the Sandline controversy. I wasn't very bothered about John Kerr's managerial criticism as I knew the talented but inexperienced young men and women coming into the press office appreciated having a boss who was too busy to crowd them, but had a good enough nose to sniff when they needed support and protection, better still some timely advice before protection was needed.

My note continues:

'Yesterday morning I was picked up at 5.30am. We flew to Cahors with Blair, Hoon and Straw [Defence and Home Secretary], where a band greeted us in the sunny square. What a nice town. I had little to do, but to catch up with paper (for the first time in this job, I think, I have no weekend reading). I bought a pair of shoes and had a lunch of duck and red wine in a brasserie.

During a break in the Cahors talks, Tony Blair stopped to say hello. He looked dreadful – his face a stretched mask of tension, his eyes blazingly focused, as if horrified by the spectacle of Mandelson. Alastair too looks lined and drained.

Blair asked what the media were doing and I said they weren't much interested in the Cahors agenda. The bulletins were leading with Peter Mandelson.

'Why's he doing this? What do you make of it?'

I said: 'It's terribly sad.'

'Sad, yes' he said. 'But irritating, too. Why's he doing it?'

His face must ache with the tension in his jaw.

He asked me what else was happening. I said we were starting to get the usual weekend pile of questions about Keith Vaz.

'Come over here,' he said.

We went to a quiet corner. 'What are they asking?'

I don't think there's much doubt that Keith's dead if even one story stacks up – so far none has, quite. I went through the latest.

Tony Blair gazed into the middle distance with that gaunt look.

'How much damage is this doing us, do you think?'

'The *Telegraph* poll is amazing today – 21 points ahead, after all this.'

'Can you believe it?'

I well remember Tony refusing to believe the polls before the last election. [As a journalist, I had been on the Blair bus throughout the 1997 election.]

He said: 'What are people making of it all, do you think?'

'They're not interested in the rights and wrongs, but they hate the spectacle.'

'You mean – we're as bad as the other lot.'

'I remember four years ago that was what you most feared – getting to that position. Phil Stephens said to Robin the other day that it took Thatcher's people 12 years to get into this state, but you've taken three years.' [Philip Stephens was chief political commentator of the *Financial Times*]

Blair looked appalled, but not surprised.

I said: 'It's not that bad.'

He took no notice, but carried on gazing gauntly. He doesn't seem to want optimistic opinions.

'So what do we do then?'

'Be positive. Your speech yesterday was really good.'

No reaction. He doesn't want praise.

'Keep doing things like that, but more important

still, play a tight game. Don't give the media any
chance to attack.'
  'Quite right.'
  Then he moved away.'

But in government you can't always play a tight game.
Something happens. You have to deal with it. What happened
was an outbreak of foot and mouth disease. The danger with
a problem like foot and mouth – so serious that people were
forbidden from country walks – is if government seems to
lose control as normal life breaks down. The Ministry of
Agriculture was not inspiring national confidence. Alastair
Campbell rang and asked if he could borrow a thoroughly
competent former journalist I had recruited, David Shaw, to
go over there and write for the Agriculture Minister.
  Robin was forgivably focused on what this meant for
him, as we all are in life. After a Sunday morning interview
with Alistair Stewart at ITN, Robin said it looked as though
things were bad enough for the election to be delayed for
a few weeks. For him, delay meant risk to the position he
built for himself, as the Foreign Secretary who would be reappointed. He wanted the election and reshuffle done before
anything could go wrong.

  'April 29, 2001
  The week before last, Robin made a speech on
  Britishness. It was obvious from a first glance at
  David Clark's draft that there were two potential
  stories: our Britishness is strengthened, not
  weakened by Europe; the multicultural nature of
  Britain is one of our strengths. The second was the
  stronger-looking story.
    This was on Tuesday, 17th. David and I agreed

to get a passage from Robin which could be trailed on Wednesday; the speech was on the Thursday. By Wednesday, though, there was violence in the Middle East and it was clear that Robin needed to do and say something, or be criticised for not doing so (we were just back from a short Easter break). Robin did a round of phone calls to Peres [Israeli foreign minister], Shaath [foreign spokesman for the PLO], Powell, etc and we set up a little media appearance for 2pm.

I was supposed to be seeing him at 1.45 and went to the park with Bradshaw for a quick snack [David Bradshaw, my former deputy at the *Daily Mirror*, now working for Tony Blair]. We ordered baked potatoes. Before they came, Lyn [Rossiter, Robin's diary secretary] rang and said: 'Where are you? The boss wants you now.' I hurried back hungry, leaving David to try to eat both spuds.

As we were preparing his statement, which needed careful drafting, it occurrred to Robin to ask about the speech – was there a story in it worth trailing, did I think?

I showed him what has now become a notorious passage.

'I'll need to re-work this,' he said.

When I came back to do the Israel media, David Clark was going through the race passage with Robin, getting him to clear it for trailing. David said: 'Jack Straw [then Home Secretary] has agreed the multicultural passage, except the reference to Chicken Tikka Masala.'

This passage described Chicken Tikka Massala as 'a true British national dish, not only because it is the most popular, but because it is a perfect illustration of the way Britain absorbs and adapts external influences.'

The speech was David Clark's lead, while I was the lead advisor on media comments about Israel and Palestine. Keeping the distinction between government and party issues can be difficult, especially when your minister is working on both at once, and each needs to be weighed against the other for the likely – and potentially competing – news impact. Robin simply wanted my view on anything he did publicly. Some issues were matters for both party and government, most obviously Europe. It was a huge strategic issue for the country, as well as highly sensitive within the Labour Party and between Labour and the Conservatives. I never gave a view on what Robin wanted to say about Conservative policy, on Europe or anything else. But I had to give a view on how his statements were positioning the government. A speech about multiculturalism was in this penumbra. Parts of David Clark's draft were partisan between Labour and the Conservatives, but the Foreign Secretary's views on Britain's multi-cultural society were a matter for government as well as party. I thought the observation about changing tastes in takeaway food a neat way of talking about multicultural Britain. I failed to see it as a risky thing to say in a party context because I wasn't thinking about that. So I failed to play my yes-but role.

> 'Robin said he wasn't sure about it either. What did I think? I said he should leave it in, as a good way of saying something that connected with real people's lives. It struck me as a bit daring, but not

dangerous.

This all took at most a minute, in amongst
working on a big, difficult foreign policy issue.
David took the passage away and said he would
brief it round. This was the right division of labour.
I spent the rest of the afternoon on Israel.

I still didn't see it as a danger, but as an opportunity
for Robin to make an important point, which had
been cleared within government. It never occurred
to me actually to say at any time – is this cleared
with Alastair Campbell?

It ran third or fourth on the early bulletins and
when Robin came down to prepare for the breakfast
programmes he asked how I thought it was going.

'Perhaps you'd better find out what Alastair
thinks.'

I got the duty press officer to check, while Robin
and I got the line right and he started doing his
interviews.

The word came back that Alastair thought the
multicultural stuff was good, he didn't like the
Chicken Tikka line. Robin did the interviews,
which were all fine. You can tell by the line of
questioning if the broadcasters think you've got a
problem, in which case you have. But they didn't.
And there was no problem. We got the backing
of both the *Mirror* and the *Sun* (I had mentioned
to Robin a couple of times that The Sun has been
doing leaders against racism), *The Guardian* and
Independent. People were calling it a brave and
honourable speech. Robin has rarely got such a
good press: few ministers do. I wrote him a note
saying it showed he was one of the few politicians

capable of making the weather and one of the few who dared be anything other than bland.

I still believe all that. It was a principled speech which only a politician of substance and conviction would make. It is the kind of thing this government should do more of – lead opinion in a way calculated to make a better country. The only people likely to be offended are those from whom we should be wresting the consensus.

The speech hadn't been cleared with Number Ten. Not only was Alastair angry, but so was Blair himself, not with the content but that he had been taken by surprise.

I was angry too. I can't understand why David Clark does these things. He knows how much work Robin has put into being a team player, how close he is to getting his reward, how (in Hugo Young's phrase) Robin has become Blair's indispensible Foreign Secretary. You can blow that kind of trust very quickly.

David Clark told Jonathan Powell he [David] was to blame.

It looked like no harm done, especially as the reception was good. But last Sunday evening I took a call from the *Telegraph*, who had been briefed that the speech ran counter to Gordon Brown's strategy of keeping out of the race row while the Tories hurt each other. It led the paper – a vicious piece of stiletto work.

David Mathieson told me David Clark had deliberately not cleared it because 'he didn't want the Brownies at Millbank to censor it'.'

The speech is worth re-reading many years later, without the limiting perspective of the day's media-political rough-house. It began:

> '*Tonight I want to celebrate Britishness. As Foreign Secretary I see every day the importance of our relations with foreign countries to the strength of our economy, to the security of our nation, to the safety of our people against organised crime, even to the health of our environment. A globalised world demands more foreign contacts than even Britain has experienced in the past.*
>
> *I also know that we are likely to make our way more successfully in the world if we are secure in our British identity, and confident about its future. That security and confidence is important for the inner strength it gives us in our conduct of business with others. I want to argue the case why we can be confident about the strength and the future of British identity. Sadly, it has become fashionable for some to argue that British identity is under siege, perhaps even in a state of terminal decline. The threat is said to come in three forms.*
>
> *First, the arrival of immigrants who, allegedly, do not share our cultural values and who fail to support the England cricket team. Few dare to state this case explicitly, but it is the unmistakable subliminal message.*
>
> *Second, our continued membership of the European Union, which is said to be absorbing member states into 'a country called Europe'.*
>
> *Third, the devolution of power to Scotland, Wales and Northern Ireland, which is seen as a*

step to the break-up of the UK.

This evening, I want to set out the reasons for being optimistic about the future of Britain and Britishness. Indeed, I want to go further and argue that in each of the areas where the pessimists identify a threat, we should instead see developments that will strengthen and renew British identity.'

The controversial passage on mutli-culturalism said:

'The idea that Britain was a 'pure' Anglo-Saxon society before the arrival of communities from the Caribbean, Asia and Africa is fantasy. But if this view of British identity is false to our past, it is false to our future too. The global era has produced population movements of a breadth and richness without parallel in history.

Today's London is a perfect hub of the globe. It is home to over 30 ethnic communities of at least 10,000 residents each. In this city tonight, over 300 languages will be spoken by families over their evening meal at home.

This pluralism is not a burden we must reluctantly accept. It is an immense asset that contributes to the cultural and economic vitality of our nation.

Legitimate immigration is the necessary and unavoidable result of economic success, which generates a demand for labour faster than can be met by the birth-rate of a modern developed country. Every country needs firm but fair immigration laws. There is no more evil business than trafficking in human beings and nothing corrodes social cohesion worse than a furtive underground of illegal migrants beyond legal protection against exploitation. But we must also create an open and inclusive society that welcomes incomers for their contribution to our growth and prosperity. Our measures to attract specialists in information technology is a good example.

Our cultural diversity is one of the reasons why Britain continues to be the preferred location for multinational companies setting up in Europe. The national airline of a major European country has recently relocated its booking operation to London precisely because of the linguistic variety of the staff whom it can recruit here.

And it isn't just our economy that has been enriched by the arrival of new communities. Our lifestyles and cultural horizons have also been broadened in the process. This point is perhaps more readily understood by young Britons, who are more open to new influences and more likely to have been educated in a multi-ethnic environment. But it reaches into every aspect of our national life.

Chicken Tikka Massala is now a true British national dish, not only because it is the most popular, but because it is a perfect illustration of the way Britain absorbs and adapts external influences. Chicken Tikka is an Indian dish. The Massala sauce was added to satisfy the desire of British people to have their meat served in gravy.

Coming to terms with multiculturalism as

a positive force for our economy and society will have significant implications for our understanding of Britishness.

The modern notion of national identity cannot be based on race and ethnicity, but must be based on shared ideals and aspirations. Some of the most successful countries in the modern world, such as the United States and Canada, are immigrant societies. Their experience shows how cultural diversity, allied to a shared concept of equal citizenship, can be a source of enormous strength. We should draw inspiration from their experience.'

The speech concluded:

'It is natural for every nation to be proud of its identity. We should be proud to be British. But we should be proud of the real Britain of the modern age.

Proud that the strength of the British character reflects the influences of the many different communities who have made their home here over the centuries. Proud that openness, mutual respect and generosity of spirit are essential British values.

We should be proud that those British values have made Britain a successful multi-ethnic society. We should welcome that pluralism as a unique asset for Britain in a modern world where our prosperity, our security and our influence depend on the health of our relations with other peoples around the globe.

171

> *Tolerance is important, but it is not enough. We should celebrate the enormous contribution of the many communities in Britain to strengthening our economy, to supporting our public services, and to enriching our culture and cuisine. And we should recognise that its diversity is part of the reason why Britain is a great place to live.'*

With the judgement of hindsight, I would say that Robin Cook and his speechwriter on this text, David Clark, deserved praise rather than blame for setting a rare standard of civilised and thoughtful political discourse. It is a pity that then and since few politicians have had the courage to speak with such intelligence and generosity and gratitude about multi-ethnic Britain. David Clark ought to have been credited and supported at the time. The episode reflects poorly on those of us who had a narrower perspective. And if this speech was a factor in Robin's demise, that is an indictment on those who contributed to and took the decision.

Ten
Shuffled Out

Once an election is called, ministerial activity ceases. They hit the road as MPs seeking re-election. Government can make statements only about urgent matters that arise. Robin dropped in during the campaign to talk to officials about foreign policy in the government's second term, including Gibraltar, on which he intended to launch a diplomatic initiative. He had no reason to doubt that he would remain Foreign Secretary. I wrote:

> 'Robin went off for the election in good political health. In every speculative piece about the post-election reshuffle, he was regarded as certain to come back as Foreign Secretary; it is not complacency to write that with five days to go, but a description of media consensus. Of course it could all go wrong.
>
> Robin told me the other day that he had sat down with his political advisors at the start of the campaign and agreed one overriding aim – no gaffes. He said he didn't want to be blamed for a mistake, particularly with Brown in charge of the campaign.
>
> We were discussing Europe at the time and, when I said this would obviously be the key issue of the second term, he said the key issue would be

'who comes out on top between Blair and Brown and I'm afraid it's slipping towards Brown'.

Last Sunday, Blair did a telephone session with callers ringing in after a PPB [Party Political Broadcast]. He asked Robin and others to be there to advise him.

Robin said: 'You know, it was striking that none of us were Brown people. It was me, Chris Smith and Steve Byers. There's a definite divide now between the Brown and Blair people. This is not good for the next parliament.'

Robin will be operating on the front line in this battle, over Europe.

He came in on Wednesday ('Gordon is keeping me out of it as much as he can') to discuss how to play Europe in the next parliament, if he comes back. He's started to say 'if', I think superstitiously rather than because he has any real doubts. Kerr says it's 100 per cent, but that's obviously an overestimate. I'd say 90.

Robin had already asked me, on the plane back from Budapest [the last engagement before the campaign, a NATO conference], to think about how to deal with the euro.

My advice to him, sitting in his room with the sun shining and only Mark Sedwill and Andrew Patrick [private secretaries] present, was to say – we said there'd be no bounce and there will be no bounce, the decision will be taken within two years. But then he should carve out a position for himself as follows. We now have a period in which to build support for Europe. It's time to grow up, calm down, chill out and get serious about Europe.

There isn't going to be a superstate, but a Europe of nations. There's a debate on its future. We're in that debate and should be confident about it. Why do the sceps work on the unpatriotic assumption we'll lose the debate? Let's put their phantoms behind us and get on with being a European power. This is the necessary platform for a referendum.

We kicked this around for an hour or so, and then he asked me to draft a speech for the Tuesday after the election, and set up a media event around it. I gave him a first draft the following day, on the theme of Britain 'at home in Europe....time to approach the issue with new confidence....time to recognise that modern Britain's power and prosperity are built on a key role in Europe'.

As the conversation wound on, he said: 'Of course, this is all very useful for now, but there will have to come a time when I become more forward leaning on the euro. That will have to be judged with great tactical care. Perhaps, if he can stay awake on June 8, I will try to discuss with the PM whether he would want me to have that role.'

He reminded me not to forget Mandelson as a factor: 'We can expect a major Mandelson speech on Europe. He and Brown will continue to wage their vendetta.'

I made a plea for getting everything squared with Number Ten and reminded him of the Tikka episode. He agreed, but said: 'We must not let Number Ten stop us speaking on Europe.'

So, if he does come back, we can expect him to be pushing at the edges of Europe policy.

Given where we started ('can I recover – and

don't bullshit me?') we've come a mighty long way and much further than Robin's detractors in Cabinet, FCO and media can (even now) quite believe. When I answered that question 'yes' back then, I wasn't sure if I was right. The question now is – what can he achieve in, presumably, two more years?'

Reshuffles are a quiet sort of agony. There is nothing to be done but wait. The power is with the Prime Minister, who calls people in when he's ready to place them in the jigsaw. It must be unbearably tense for the men and women whose careers – all they have dreamed of and worked for – hang on a summons to Number Ten. The victim or beneficiary is rarely consulted, merely told.

When Robin Cook went into Number Ten that day after the 2001 election, he had had no warning of what to expect. This is my note written a couple of days later.

'Robin was booked to see the Prime Minister at 4.15pm. It slipped to 4.45pm. It came up on PA [news agency] that he had gone in. I had been pretty tense all day, because you can't take life for granted. Right up to the end there wasn't a trace of doubt in the newspaper predictions that Robin would stay at the FCO, except that Don Macintyre [political commentator, *Independent*] had said that certainly Prescott would go to the Cabinet Office and Robin (almost certainly) stay where he was. I said to Pat: 'Don doesn't open and close brackets lightly – I wonder if he's picked something up there.' Still I didn't worry too much; only kept reminding myself that in every reshuffle there is something unexpected.

Lesley [Beats: I had two secretaries at that time] came in and said there was a rumour that Robin was gone, and that we were getting a new Foreign Secretary. About 6.30 Sherard rang and said: 'You've probably heard that Robin Cook has been sacked and we're getting Jack Straw. Cook has been given ten minutes to decide whether to accept Leader of the House.'

Phil Webster [*The Times*] rang, having heard the same thing, but that Robin had accepted. I said I wasn't going to steer him off it, but I hadn't been told officially yet.

At 7.15 Lesley took a call and said: 'You're to go upstairs and see Robin Cook.'

He was standing by his desk, drinking brandy. Robin looked as though he had been roughed up.

I said: 'I'm sorry. You didn't deserve this.'

He shook his head, as if to brush regrets aside.

I said: 'You deserved better.'

Sherard said: 'The three of us have failed in our central objective.'

I said: 'No we haven't.'

I don't regard Sherard as a joint owner of the Cook objectives. I was thinking back to the first serious conversation I had with Robin in this great, pompous room, when he had asked if he could survive.

He was recognised long before he finished as a class act, a really competent and wily Foreign Secretary who delivered for Britain. Nobody can take that away from him. I told him so.

He took a call, about the complicated consequences of giving up or not giving up his official accommodation, and rang Number Ten to bring them up to date. He said to the switchboard: 'Hello, it's the Foreign Secretary.'

And while he waited to be put through he said: 'I find myself wanting to use the title for as long as I can. Mind you, the new title isn't a bad one – Lord President of the Council. You realise I am president of the Privy Council now.'

He was mocking himself. During his conversation with Number Ten, they must have mentioned official cars because he said: 'I'm not sure the answer to that, because I've had a couple of brandies and so I couldn't drive myself anyway'.

He looked up and said: 'You realise I lose my close protection.'

Only the PM, Foreign, Home and Northern Ireland Secretaries have security. Some hate it, but the policemen are nice blokes and I've always had the impression Robin likes having them around.

You could feel it dawning on him.

He said: 'Life's too short for bitterness, but it is unjust.'

(I reminded him of that this morning when he rang and began to sound bitter. I said: 'I admired you for saying that on Friday night because it certainly wasn't how I felt.')

His immediate problem on Friday night was how to handle the story.

He said: 'As one last favour, could you advise me what to do?'

I said: 'Do the bulletins. If you go to ground, it will look terrible. And I'll tell Phil [Webster] and others that you're a House of Commons man who looks forward to spending more time in parliament, which you've missed.'

The Times splash reflected that high up in the story.

We fixed for Robin to do a little stand-up at I Carlton Gardens at nine. I was relieved to hear from Sherard that Jack wouldn't be coming in tonight. It meant I could devote the evening to Robin.

As I was walking across the park to 1CG, Jack's special advisor Ed Owen rang. He put Jack on the line. Jack said he was looking forward to working together.

He asked how Robin was and said it had come as a shock to him. Jack said he would want to make a statement next day which paid a proper tribute to Robin. Could I work on it?

At 1CG, I waited for Robin in the upstairs sitting room where we've plotted many a media performance and prepared for many a battle. It was in that room that we faced up to the horrible problem we had when it was clear that Robin had a choice between admitting in a parliamentary answer that Ernie Ross had supplied us with a leaked copy of Sandline report; or quit rather than shop his old friend. He had made clear he would rather quit. Fortunately, Ernie said there was no point hiding it and owned up. That was among the top three bad moments of that nightmare period before Robin soared away from his problems and became a big figure again.

He came down. The obvious line – usually the best – hadn't occurred to him. I said: 'Call yourself a House of Commons man because it's the kind of cliche they'll use.'

He did it with his usual professionalism, though I thought he couldn't help looking unhappy.

As ever, we went upstairs to talk about how he'd done, but quickly moved on to what had happened. He seemed unsure why it had happened.

I said: 'Didn't the Prime Minister give you a reason?'

'He only said he wanted a big change.'

Robin said he suspected Anji Hunter's influence [a senior advisor to Tony Blair]. He said he also suspected Kerr had been working against him. I said that during the election I had noticed Kerr and the machine treating me 'a bit provisionally, as if they think they might yet get rid of me along with you'. It was all piffling stuff, like refusing to discuss the problem I have with my deputy until after the election, but it was all of a piece .

He said that if I felt that way I was welcome to go with him: let him know soon, though.

By the time I left, it was getting on for ten. It was dark on the grand stairway. He thanked me again for everything I'd done and I wished him well. I said: 'I'm sure you'll do it well. You'd do anything well.'

I hadn't much doubt that I wanted to stay on at the Foreign Office. It's a great job, despite the frustration and the snobbery. I love the travel.

In the morning, Robin rang and I took him through the papers. They were pretty cruel, reporting his move as a demotion, but all reflected shock, a recognition of his quality, his contributions to Kosovo and Nice, and the intriguing prospect of the greatest parliamentarian of the day leading the Commons. I spared him the worst, but dwelt at length on *The Mirror* leader saying he was the one person with the guts to tell the country what it needs.

He was in a bad way.

'Watch your back,' he said. 'Michael Levy [Labour donor, friend of Blair, Middle East envoy] says he's heard Foreign Office officials were lobbying Number Ten that if I was coming back only for a couple of years, I might as well go now.'

I told him how Kerr had suspected me – and therefore Robin – of briefing against Number Ten last autumn. This is one of several small factors which – I'm convinced – combined to do for Robin.

On Sunday, Robin rang again to discuss the papers, but this time he'd read most of them. He hadn't noticed a leader in *The Independent* on Sunday saying he had the chance of a place in history if he used his parliamentary skills to restore the standing of the Commons.

He said: 'I'm thinking I'll work through this long session to the autumn of 2002 and then, ahead of the next reshuffle, let it be known I'm retiring. I'd like an international job, or to go into consultancy. But whatever I do my market value declines if I fall out with Tony.'

I suggested he be more careful in briefing the media. He said he hadn't been able to get hold of his press officer, who was in any case only temporary. He'd asked David Mathieson to ring round.

He talked about starting on his memoirs and asked for advice on how to get an agent. I said I'd be happy to help him write them.

During the afternoon, the *Today* programme rang to say they didn't know how to get hold of Robin. I rang him.

'Do you think I should do it?'

'They'll be interested only in the euro.'

'I think I'll do it.'

'Are you sure you want to get into that?'

'Yes. I'm not bitter, but I do feel a steely anger. I'm sick of some junior press officer at Number Ten telling me not to do the Today programme (a reference, I presume, to the row with Tim Livesey that night in Marseille when Robin refused to stay off the air). I've given these people four years of absolute loyalty and look what it's got me.'

Peter Hain told me he thought the Chicken Tikka speech had cost Robin the job. I think it was only one of several incidents and factors, though I very much regretted not having spotted the problem and warned against. A week after Robin's departure I reflected in a note:

> 'I'm convinced now that he built up too much of a nuisance factor and that is probably why he went. When the reshuffle jigsaw didn't quite fit, the PM didn't have quite enough commitment to keeping him, because he had too often irritated Number Ten. There were the occasional outbursts, especially the *Sunday Telegraph* story last November when a source close to Robin told Brown to get his tanks off our lawn. There was Chicken Tikka. And above all there was the persistent pushing at the limits of euro policy,

chiefly on that day when we mistakenly handed
out a speech text which Number Ten had censored
at the last minute at Brown's behest.'

This was a farcical incident in which I had, as was common
practice, handed out the Foreign Secretary's text for the
media to check against delivery, as he rose to speak in a
Commons debate. It had some enthusiastic phrases about
the euro, none of them breaking a policy line, but between
them giving a deliberately strong impression of support for
entry. Robin hadn't got far when I started noticing that he
was skipping these phrases. The lobby immediately realised
what must have happened. I hurried down to Robin's room
afterwards to find that the Chancellor had at the last moment
sent back his comments on the text, deleting phrase after
phrase. There was no disguising what had happened. The
story just had to run its course, to my intense embarrassment.
In fact, the lobby decided this must have been a wickedly
cunning tactic to obey but not obey, to delete as ordered,
while giving out the real text accidentally on purpose. Robin
and I didn't do cunning.

Robin's problem was that he too often let himself say what
he meant. It is neither trivial nor cynical that politicians need to
be careful about that, and to have people like me to warn them
where the boundary is. They are members of a Cabinet which
is collectively responsible for the government's policies, on
which they are answerable to parliament and the electorate.
If they want to have different views, there is plenty of room
on the backbenches, and Robin showed in the end that he was
big enough to make that choice over Iraq. If ministers freely
contradicted each other all the time, the public would not be
able to tell what the policy is and therefore whether to vote
for or against. But anyone who has intelligence, beliefs and

character must find it uncomfortable to be 'on message' all the time. Robin did make serious efforts to tilt the argument in favour of the euro against the Chancellor's cautious policy, but not always in the most calculated way. He had two major issues in which he was always wrestling with himself, the euro and arms sales.

His government career was nearly ended prematurely by farce as much as by policy differences, and thereafter the Foreign Secretary was often defending his dignity as much as his principles. He emerged with both intact, and with serious achievements which live up to his declared intention to have a foreign policy with an ethical dimension, though this memoir has not tried to justify that phrase. It was a mistake to use words that set an unachievable standard, giving critics and enemies – of which Robin had a few – a line to ridicule him with. We do not have a politics in which a minister can set high aims, without inviting scorn, when things go wrong, as they do.

But we do have a politics in which a minister can, with enough persistence, make the compromises and take the batterings that are necessary in a parliamentary democracy, accommodate the limitations of power in practice, and by the quality of his work and the decency of his character, make something worthwhile of his short time in office. Robin Cook's legacy includes the International Criminal Court, not mentioned in my notes at the time, so missing from the narrative. But it is hard to see how the Court could have been created against US opposition without strong support from Britain. It fitted exactly Robin's views that states must be held accountable for criminal acts. Tony Blair was not enthusiastic. I remember being in the Foreign Secretary's office at a critical point in the negotiation of the Rome Treaty, which created the Court. He was on the phone to our lead negotiator and said – sign. Robin turned to me and said: 'I don't think I need to consult Tony about that.'

His legacy includes a share of responsibility for the relative stability of the Balkans, a stronger and more comfortable role for Britain in the enlarged Europe that he worked hard for, as well as in a policy of critical engagement with Libya and Iran, which had important specific outcomes that were very much worth having. These were not achieved by Robin Cook alone – international relations don't work like that – but none would have happened without the intelligent and creative application of his principles, in action. It is a good hand of achievements by any standards, but especially so for someone who had first to survive an ordeal by media, of an intensity that few politicians have been through. There is nothing wrong with subjecting power to criticism, even to scorn if justified. For democracy to work as an effective system of government, politicians sometimes have to be strong and decent enough to stay upright in a media storm.

Robin Cook was never an entirely comfortable fit in the Blair-Brown government, but was a great asset to it, not only for his fine intelligence but because – I think – people sensed a man of principle. He was not alone in being a strong character, with principles. The same applied to his successor, Jack Straw. But Jack was politically closer to Blair, and on the euro closer to Brown, than Robin had been.

There was one thing in common to these two Foreign Secretaries for whom I worked closely. Having mastered the job after early difficulties, they both developed a distinctive edge to their foreign policy, taking firm positions of their own choosing rather than simply following the Prime Minister's lead. And this was a Prime Minister who liked to lead on foreign policy.

I concluded my last note about working for Robin Cook:

'I don't think any one small thing did for Robin, but one big thing did. For all his many qualities, his awkward public personality made him dispensible. Robin's extreme competence ought to have been enough. But it wasn't. He carried too many negatives about with him. The feud with Brown was fatal. Number Ten could simply do without the aggro, the tension with the Treasury, the constant niggling over the euro (remember Robin saying it was 'inevitable', remember his Japan speech when Alastair said – is this deliberate?). I am conscious now that he's gone that I lived my life in a chronic state of fretfulness over what trouble we'd be trying to avoid or get out of next. There must have been the same feeling in Number Ten, that Robin was a constant worry, despite being consistently excellent at his job.

On Thursday, Robin flew with some of us to Gothenburg [to the EU summit] to preside over the Party of European Socialists' meeting, while Jack flew with the PM. It was terribly sad to see him back among the trappings of the great office, sitting in his usual seat on the plane, painfully aware of what he had lost.

He's not finished. He had a standing ovation at the Parliamentary Labour Party meeting and was, apparently, dazzling in Cabinet when he presented the legislative programme. He could yet finish a big figure, admired and held in affection as a principled individualist. But it will take a very big man to pull round and achieve that after what they have done to him.'

Eleven
After

As the Foreign Office Press Secretary and Director of Communications, I stayed in post working for the new Foreign Secretary, Jack Straw. Working for the Foreign Secretary leaves little time for much else, and Cabinet ministers' offices are separate compartments, so I lost touch with Robin Cook. He and Gaynor came to Pam and my 25th wedding anniversary, which fell on 11th September 2001, though we had our party the Sunday before. What happened on that 11th September accelerated and intensified everything to do with foreign policy. Though I closely followed Robin Cook's efforts to reform the House of Lords, hoping that could be a fine legacy for his parliamentary career, I did so as a spectator, and saw nothing of him, other than occasionally passing in a corridor. I recall a brief hello as Robin came out of a Cabinet as I was waiting for Jack Straw, on one of the last occasions when Iraq was discussed before the decision for war. I never discussed the Iraq war with Robin, and had no reason to. Had I shared his doubts about the policy, I would have raised them with the current Foreign Secretary.

I did not have such doubts. I regret that failure. Having consistently played the 'yes, but' role on all sorts of issues, I never raised a hand and said – yes, but are we sure Iraq has weapons of mass destruction? I have since asked myself many hard questions about why not. I answered them in written evidence to the inquiry into the war chaired by Sir John Chilcott:

> 'People now find it hard to believe that anyone involved in Iraq policy was not aware of the wrongness of building a case on non-existent weapons of mass destruction. How did we not realise? One reason that I did not realise – as well as my points above about my respect for the judgement of key officials – was that Tony Blair had been right about Kosovo against the prevailing wisdom. Some in the media argued for 78 consecutive days that bombing could not win that conflict, and when on day 79 it did, they moved on without acknowledgement. Having seen Tony Blair's instincts vindicated in adversity – in my view – I was inclined to believe he was right again.'

The key word is 'judgement'. The challenges of foreign policy look far less clearcut – right and wrong – when going into them forwards than they do looking backwards after the event. My judgement on the Iraq war was wrong. As I wrote to the Chilcott inquiry: 'I had never imagined for a moment that of all the outcomes of this intense process, the truth would be that Iraq had no weapons of mass destruction.'

Robin Cook did foresee that outcome, and having made that judgement, he resigned. It had not been clairvoyance that made me say to him, two years before, that he would end up resigning on as issue of principle. It was a reading of political character, that for Robin government was a struggle to reconcile principles with the democratic necessity to compromise – a constant judgement of where the line is: to concede and stay to fight for core beliefs, or to decide that the line has been crossed, and leave. Robin Cook made very clear where the line was for him on Iraq, and when the government crossed it, he resigned.

I very much regret on a personal level that I saw nothing of him during this period. There was no political reason for this. He and Jack Straw had a good personal relationship and I recall not a single moment in which I felt there was any friction. I have no insight into Robin's thinking as he moved towards resignation. I was only aware as everyone in politics and the media was aware, that Robin Cook had reservations about the direction Iraq policy was taking.

His resignation speech was scheduled immediately before a Commons statement by Jack Straw on the situation. Jack respected Robin's decision and the openness with which he had reached it, so had no intention of getting into an argument with his predecessor. The speech that I helped Jack Straw to write was about the end of the diplomatic process on which he had been tirelessly engaged, having believed until the end that war might be avoided by United Nations pressure on Saddam Hussein to allow open inspections. My hindsight view, having worked for both Foreign Secretaries, is that they were as sincere as one another about Iraq.

So I went up into the House of Commons press gallery to watch them both, and made this note afterwards.

'The Labour benches were packed with rebels, and Robin's small but conspicuous presence on the backbenches silently dominated the House. I swear he was sitting just where Geoffrey Howe sat as he waited to make his resignation statement. This was an occasion of similar scale. Although Blair is now more dominant than Thatcher was in her twilight years, it was nevertheless impossible to imagine her being brought down, until Howe's speech. So what damage would Robin do to Blair?

Robin was good – stylish, compelling, persuasive. His best line was that if the hanging chads in Florida had gone the other way, we would not be where we are.

Robin's resignation was a great parliamentary occasion, and his the best case against war that I've heard. I'm pleased for him. I thought back to the day I started work for him, and he said – am I finished, no bullshitting? This is the best course for Robin.'

A decade on, there is another passage that stands out. As we had discussed on his last night as Foreign Secretary, Robin was a House of Commons man. And characteristically, he finished on a reflection on the importance of Parliament and of the accountability of Members to the people they serve.

The longer that I have served in this place, the greater the respect I have for the good sense and collective wisdom of the British people.

On Iraq, I believe that the prevailing mood of the British people is sound. They do not doubt that Saddam is a brutal dictator, but they are not persuaded that he is a clear and present danger to Britain. They want inspections to be given a chance, and they suspect that they are being pushed too quickly into conflict by a US Administration with an agenda of its own. Above all, they are uneasy at Britain going out on a limb on a military adventure without a broader international coalition and against the hostility of many of our traditional allies.

From the start of the present crisis, I have insisted, as Leader of the House, on the right of this place to vote on whether Britain should go to war. It has been a favourite theme of commentators that this House no longer occupies a central role in British politics. Nothing could better demonstrate that they are wrong than for this House to stop the commitment of troops in a war that has neither international agreement nor domestic support.

I intend to join those tomorrow night who will vote against military action now. It is for that reason, and for that reason alone, and with a heavy heart, that I resign from the government.